The Totality of Allegiance

The Totality of Allegiance

Inside the Hearts and Minds of Trump Supporters

Travis Ruddle
&
Brad Agle

Copyright © 2024 by Travis Ruddle and Brad Agle

All rights reserved.

No part of this publication may be reproduced, stored in a retrieval system or transmitted in any form or by any means, electronic, mechanical, photocopying, recording, or otherwise, without the prior permission of the publisher or in accordance with the provisions of the Copyright, Designs and Patents Act 1988 or under the terms of any license permitting limited copying issued by the Copyright Licensing Agency.

Published in the United States by Freedom Peak Press LLC, Utah

Publisher's Cataloging-in-Publication Data

Names: Ruddle, Travis, author. | Agle, Bradley R., author.
Title: The totality of allegiance : inside the hearts and minds of Trump supporters / Travis Ruddle & Brad Agle.
Description: Includes bibliographical references and index. | Provo, UT: Freedom Peak Press, 2024.
Identifiers: LCCN: 2024920830 | ISBN: 979-8-9916708-0-7 (paperback) | 979-8-9916708-1-4 (epub)
Subjects: LCSH Trump, Donald, 1946- --Influence. | Right-wing extremists--United States. | Political culture--United States. | Social conflict--Political aspects--United States. | Identity politics--United States. | Polarization (Social sciences)--United States. | United States--Social conditions--21st century. | Populism. | BISAC POLITICAL SCIENCE / Political Ideologies / Democracy | POLITICAL SCIENCE / Political Ideologies / General | POLITICAL SCIENCE / Political Ideologies / Fascism & Totalitarianism
Classification: LCC JK1764 .R84 2024 | DDC 306.20973 --dc23
LC record available at https://lccn.loc.gov/2024920830

Cover Design: Travis Ruddle
Book Design: Alyssa Farnsworth

totalityofallegiance.com

Printed in the United States of America

*To the pursuit of knowledge and
the ones who make it possible*

CONTENTS

	Authors' Notes	11
	Introduction	25
Chapter 1.	The Research Study	35
Chapter 2.	The Trump Phenomenon	47
Chapter 3.	Moral Rationalization	59
Chapter 4.	Tribalism	73
Chapter 5.	Victimhood	87
Chapter 6.	Conmen, Cults, and Those Who Follow	99
Chapter 7.	Authoritarianism and the Strongman	113
Chapter 8.	Evaluating Fact and Fiction	127
Chapter 9.	Avoiding and Overcoming *The Totality of Allegiance*	139
	Conclusion	149
	Acknowledgments	165
	Appendix	167
	Notes	175
	Index	187

"Facts are stubborn things; and whatever may be our wishes, our inclinations, or the dictates of our passions, they cannot alter the state of facts and evidence..."
- John Adams, *Wemms Trial,* December 1770

"The ideal subject of totalitarian rule is not the convinced Nazi or the convinced Communist, but people for whom the distinction between fact and fiction (i.e., the reality of experience) and the distinction between true and false (i.e., the standards of thought) no longer exist."
- Hannah Arendt, *The Origins of Totalitarianism*

Authors' Notes

I was the odd kid in high school who appreciated politics. Engaging with diverse issues, opinions, and policies was thrilling and enlightening. The political landscape was clearly tribal based on my own upbringing, as it is typically with everyone else. However, I had an innate and undeniable motivation to explore – the other side. To me, it was important to venture beyond the conventional understanding and seek enlightenment from various viewpoints rather than from the place I currently stood. I was the student who persistently introduced political discourse into conversations or donned campaign shirts during primary and general elections, even though I was under the age to vote. I was profoundly disheartened when I could not cast my vote in the 2008 election for Senator John

McCain and Governor Sarah Palin, missing the cutoff by a mere year.

Someone, in jest, put an Obama yard sign directly on the windshield of my parked '77 Ford pickup the day after the election. At the time, I felt extremely dejected after the election loss and openly upset by what appeared to be vandalism. Though now I look back and laugh, wishing for the days when political engagement was spirited, full of passion, yet fun. Letting go of trivialities is indeed beneficial for our politics, and I have seen this erode over the last two decades in the most consequential of ways.

Yes, I was (and remain) an unusual soul who thrived on political debate and discussion. Each day after school, I would plant myself in front of the television flipping between MSNBC, CNN, and Fox News, absorbing all the information I could. The analysis and commentary often became heated, riling me up as a politically conservative youth. This channel-switching, however, forced me out of my comfort zone, exposing me to different perspectives. It empowered me to discern and recognize truths worth holding onto amidst evident facts and mingled falsehoods. Gradually, I could see the full picture, even though it was often painted and sometimes outweighed by biased commentaries devoid of evidence.

My journey continued as I transitioned from my small hometown of Adair, Oklahoma, to the University of Oklahoma in Norman. After completing my first year, I seized on the phenomenal opportunity to travel and study abroad, stepping outside the country for the first time. With just two semesters of German under my belt, I immersed myself in another culture, society, and language. This profoundly influenced my love of connecting with others who have different experiences, my desire to learn, and most of all, this inner enlightenment and ability to think critically. Taking Mark Twain's advice that "travel is fatal to prejudice, bigotry, and narrow-mindedness," I embarked on a transformative journey that was to reshape not just my worldview but also the very essence of my intellectual pursuits.[1]

My travel and experience in Germany led me to confront the highest and lowest points of human society and its history. Ettersberg Hill, outside the small city of Weimar, holds a grim paradox—the birthplace of profound cultural and intellectual achievements and the site of unimaginable human suffering. Here, at one of the largest concentration camps within Germany's pre-World War II borders, Buchenwald, a dark shadow of history looms large. In the very area where Johann Wolfgang Goethe once lived and contributed to the Enlightenment—a movement that sought to elevate reason, clarity, and the moral progress of humanity—this camp stood as a grotesque negation of those ideals. The Enlightenment, which had aimed to bring "Aufklärung" or a clear-sighted understanding of the balance between politics, society, and culture, was here, on this very soil, symbolically and practically obliterated by the establishment of the camp by the Schutzstaffel (SS) in July 1937.

As we traveled from the center of Weimar to Buchenwald, I was struck by the tragic irony: How could a land so deeply steeped in the intellectual legacy of figures like Immanuel Kant, who famously urged humanity to "Have courage to use your own understanding,"[2] also become the site of such unfathomable cruelty? It is as though the very spirit of enlightenment was forced into a dark recess, supplanted by a cold, calculated perversion of reason.

Upon arrival, I confronted a deeply unsettling reality. How could the residents of Weimar not have known the atrocities were occurring so close to their homes? How did they reconcile the camp's existence with the Enlightenment values that once flourished in their midst? As I walked through the main gate, with its cynical inscription "Jedem Das Seine" (To Each Their Own), I pondered whether those who lived nearby—those who baked bread for the camp, delivered food orders to the gate, or wandered near the encampment's border—were truly ignorant of the horrors within. Did they really believe that those interned were receiving what they "deserved," as the gate's inscription suggested? Or was the truth so obscured, so entangled in the web of propaganda and fear, that even the obvious became uncertain?

Throughout this book, I channel the philosophical spirit of Hannah Arendt, a scholar and political theorist whose insightful reflections on the nature of power, authority, and totalitarianism have deeply influenced my understanding of human behavior and one's standing in the world. Arendt's meticulous analysis of the rise of strongmen and autocratic regimes—rooted in the erosion of truth, the manipulation of facts, and the obliteration of the individual's capacity for independent thought—serves as a powerful lens through which we can examine the disturbing trends of our own time. Just as Arendt explored the terrifying consequences of a society willing to sacrifice reason for ideology, I, too, grapple with the forces that drive people away from critical thinking and one's own morals and principles and toward the seductive allure of an autocratic savior.

This book delves into the mechanisms by which truth is distorted and moral clarity is obscured—a process that Arendt identified as the hallmark of totalitarianism. We examine the historical precedents that reveal how democracies can be undermined from within, not through sudden upheaval, but through the gradual erosion of values, the normalization of falsehoods, and the insidious spread of propaganda. These are not merely abstract concerns; they are the lived experiences of countless individuals who have witnessed their societies descend into tyranny.

Faced with the moral dilemmas of our era, I find myself in the forest, trying to either retreat into silence or rise within my sphere of expertise to shed light on the disturbing parallels between the rise of totalitarianism in the 20th century and the alarming trends we witness today. The stakes are high; for history has shown us that the erosion of democratic principles can lead to catastrophic outcomes.

U.S. President John Adams famously stated that:

> *"Facts are stubborn things; and whatever may be our wishes, our inclinations, or the dictates of our passion, they cannot alter the state of facts and evidence."*[3]

When comparing Trump's America to historical periods rich with elements of authoritarianism and fascism, the parallels are too significant to overlook. The slow, seductive erosion of democracy is not merely a historical concern; it is a present danger that threatens the very foundations of our society.

In this book, I urge you to engage with these ideas critically, to reflect on the zenith of democracy, and to recognize how its foundations are being eroded—subtly, yet with potentially catastrophic consequences. The history of autocrats, demagogues, and totalitarianism is not a distant memory; it is a living, breathing threat that requires our vigilance, our courage, and our unwavering commitment to truth and ethical leadership. Only by confronting these realities can we hope to safeguard the principles of democracy for future generations.

Travis Ruddle, Ph.D.
Assistant Professor,
Romney Institute of Public Services and Ethics,
Marriott School of Business, Brigham Young University

A few months after graduating from Handy High School in Bay City, Michigan, in the spring of 1980, I arrived as a missionary for the Church of Jesus Christ of Latter-day Saints in Munich, Germany. A few weeks after arriving, while assigned to labor in the city of Landshut, approximately 70 kilometers from Munich, I had the opportunity to visit Dachau, the Nazi model and headquarters concentration camp. The experience was profound. While I had learned about the Holocaust growing up, nothing prepared me for the intense evil I felt. The buildings were left standing as a memorial to those who suffered and died there, and a warning to future generations. The evil I felt was so tangible that I distinctly remember a strong desire and need to leave. The way people had been treated was astonishing. How could people torture others, perform medical experiments on them, take everything from them, and eventually kill them?

During the hours on the train back to Landshut, I pondered upon the inhumanity inflicted on other human beings. How could such profound evil exist in the world? How could these people do what they did? Were these people genuinely malicious, or was there another explanation? Did the local townspeople know what was going on and were they complicit in it or ignorant of it? Why had they not done anything to stop what was going on there? Unbeknownst to me, and only upon future reflection did I realize that day began my journey of discovery as a social scientist.

Over the next twenty-one months living in Germany and Austria, I realized that just about anyone I met who was over the age of 50 had been involved in the Nazi regime earlier in their life. While they had not all been SS officers, members of the Gestapo, or pro-Nazi partisans, they had virtually all been at least partially active citizens during the Nazi period. While the war was not a popular topic of conversation or brought up with any regularity, now and again, I would gain a bit of insight into that time and how people thought about it. There was no question that the people had felt desperate and humiliated. Adolf Hitler had brought them hope. And while certainly a minority opinion, I sometimes even heard positive remarks about der Führer despite knowing all they knew at that point.

It also struck me that most of these older Germans were not particularly evil people. While they certainly included a variety of personalities and characters, generally, they were nice people who loved their families and their communities and were willing to serve each other. While they didn't always appreciate me trying to share what they perceived to be an American religion with them, in most interactions they were generally respectful and sometimes even charitable. Germany and Austria are beautiful countries because of the order and cleanliness they enforce and the respect they have for their fellow citizens.

Upon entering Brigham Young University in the Fall of 1982, I began formal studies with classes such as German language, culture, and history. These courses provided me with insights into my questions. In 1983, I had my first course in organizational behavior, where I learned about social science experiments designed to understand what had happened during the Holocaust from a scientific perspective. I learned about the Milgram experiments at Yale, which attempted to understand the extent to which individuals would obey an authority figure simply because of their authority role. Professor Stanley Milgram's shock experiments truly stunned the scientific community. Contrary to what leading psychologists predicted, individuals were largely willing to obey an authority figure who told them to perform a horrific act simply because of their position of authority. These studies, as well as others such as the Stanford prison experiments, provided me with a small level of insight and a thirst for greater understanding. It was in this class that I first considered earning a Ph.D. and becoming a career social scientist.

In the Fall of 1988, I felt incredibly blessed to be admitted into a new Ph.D. major at the University of Washington Business School. While the majority of Ph.D. majors cause one to become very narrow in their research, mine was in some ways quite the opposite. My expertise was seeing interactions and themes across multiple disciplines, which required me to gain a fundamental understanding of economics, history, sociology, psychology, philosophy, anthropology, law, statistics, research methods, and political science. This multidisciplinary background has served me well as I've examined the questions posed in this book.

My research over the past 35 years has focused on ethical behavior in organizations; leadership of CEOs of large organizations, and the support they do or don't receive from their followers; leader, and follower factors that cause a charismatic relationship to develop between and among them (leading to good or evil outcomes); leadership priorities involving their stakeholders; ethical role models; values and religious factors that affect leaders and followers; and the different types of ethical issues people encounter in organizational life.

From 1980 to 2015, I pondered what happened during the Third Reich through my casual study of history as well as linking my own research and the social science studies I was reading. I tell friends that for those 35 years, I was researching the rise and fall of Nazism through the study of history and social science. From 2015 until now, I have been watching that same rise of authoritarianism happening through the ascendancy of Donald Trump. Here is just one example of the parallels. Like most Americans, I am not happy about what is happening at our southern border. However, I am deeply disturbed by the dehumanization process I see Trump using against immigrants, similar to the tactics employed during the Third Reich. Hitler blamed the Jews for all of Germany's problems, called them names, claimed they were inferior in all ways to true Germans, and claimed they were vermin and a scourge on German society. There are stark differences but undeniable similarities to what Trump is currently doing regarding those seeking asylum in the United States.

Even though, as a lifelong Republican, I am not a fan of many of the policies of President Joe Biden or Vice President Kamala Harris, I was relieved when Trump was voted out of office in 2020. My expectations for Trump's behavior following his loss were not high, though I was shocked by what he wrought in the two post-election months. While lawsuits may be warranted, Trump's behavior starkly contrasts President George Washington's. During the Revolutionary War and the early years of our Republic, Washington exemplified the principles necessary for sustaining our fragile form of government—democracy.

Even though I was busy with interesting projects in August 2023, I decided I needed to put those aside while I did what I could to help our precious republic.

Meanwhile, friends and family have told me my efforts are in vain because I will not be able to make a real difference. I suspect they are correct, but I believe in the perspective of President Teddy Roosevelt that one cannot simply be a critic, but one must get in the arena and try to make a difference. For those unfamiliar with the majestic words delivered by Roosevelt at the Sorbonne, they follow:

> *"It is not the critic who counts; not the man who points out how the strong man stumbles, or where the doer of deeds could have done them better. The credit belongs to the man who is actually in the arena, whose face is marred by dust and sweat and blood; who strives valiantly; who errs, who comes short again and again, because there is no effort without error and shortcoming; but who does actually strive to do the deeds..."*[4]

I am grateful for my wonderful, brilliant, and tenacious young colleague, Travis Ruddle, who chose to join me in this work. I am also buoyed by the tremendously talented and dedicated Brigham Young University students who have worked diligently on this project. I am also grateful for the wonderful Trump supporters who agreed to join our focus groups, knowing that while attempting to be as objective in our social science work as possible, we were doing this project as non-Trump supporters.

I felt a strong need to do this project for several important reasons. First, I sought to gain a deeper understanding of whether my perception of the Trump phenomenon bearing resemblance to the Hitler phenomenon was well-founded. Second, as a trained critic holding a Ph.D., I aimed to rigorously examine and evaluate my interpretation of the facts surrounding the Trump campaign. Last, if my perspectives were indeed accurate, I intended to take measures to prevent the emergence of authoritarianism in the United States.

I did this research for the future of my four children and ten grandchildren, as well as friends, neighbors, fellow citizens in the United States, and friends around the world who are significantly affected by what happens in our country. Finally, studying Trump and his supporters has required sacrificing some of my mental and emotional health. I did this work with an understanding of the peril I put myself in. Many of the first prisoners at Dachau were political prisoners. Former President Trump has vowed to exact revenge on those he sees as his enemies. I do not doubt him.

Brad Agle, Ph.D.,
George W. Romney Endowed Professor,
Romney Institute of Public Service and Ethics,
Marriott School of Business, Brigham Young University

Introduction

The rise of Trumpism is not solely attributed to one man, but represents a significant movement driven by real people who have fundamentally changed the landscape of American politics. Often, discussions focus on Trump's policies, performance, and conduct, but the real interest should lie in understanding the mass political and social movements and the very supporters of Trump. These are the individuals who may or may not fly the MAGA flag, attend rallies, defend him at dinner tables across America, and eventually vote for him. They hold a genuine belief in this individual, and it is necessary to recognize this reality. It is essential to understand these supporters' motivations and how they process and interpret information—facts and falsehoods—in their support and defense of Trump.

What we are witnessing in Trumpism is more than political alignment; it is the crystallization of a profound allegiance that transcends policy and enters the realm of identity and belief. Our book is not just another analysis of Trump's rise but an exploration of the deeper psychological, political, sociological, and ethical currents that drive such unwavering support. This *totality of allegiance*—a commitment so encompassing that it often disregards truth and real evidence—forms the strong pillar of Donald Trump's support and necessitates respectful and deliberate attention.

To truly understand this allegiance, we conducted in-depth focus groups across the United States in South Carolina, Utah, Oklahoma, and Arizona. These focus groups involved 55 participants from diverse backgrounds. We made a concerted effort to ensure that our sample varied widely in terms of gender, age, religion, and income demographics to accurately represent the makeup of Trump supporters. Each of our participants was selected to represent a wide array of perspectives within Trump's base. The intimate setting of these focus groups allowed for thoughtful conversations, which offered unique insights into the issues discussed in this book. The data gathered from these discussions is not merely anecdotal but serves as a foundational element of our analysis, providing a human face to the theories and concepts explored in the subsequent chapters.

One of the key topics we explore is the severe distrust that Trump supporters harbor toward institutions—government, media, academia, and beyond. Citizens' distrust is not just a symptom of this period in time but a driving force behind the present political and social dynamics.

We held our very first focus group in South Carolina and it was a fantastic learning experience. During a robust discussion on authority figures such as judges, politicians, scientists, a male participant expressed forcefully:

"I'm unimpressed with smart people."

What might be an odd but nonetheless simple sentiment, the comment reflects a real and genuine skepticism toward intellectual elites and experts, which has become a significant element of Trump's new Republican Party. Anti-intellectualism and the disdain for authority figures who speak out against Trump were consistent themes in our focus groups. Those figures are not to be trusted.

This distrust is additionally fueled by years of economic challenges, perceived cultural shifts, and the belief that traditional American values are under siege. Trump's rhetoric did not create this distrust alone, but it did amplify and weaponize it, turning it into a powerful tool of political mobilization. This distrust is often coupled with a sense of victimhood, as articulated by this same participant who stated:

> *"I, as a Trump person, don't want to violate any law in Washington D.C., Massachusetts, Illinois, [or] California. But if I'm in Alabama or Tennessee or South Carolina I'll probably be okay. I might get a fair trial."*

This view reflects a deep-seated belief among some supporters that they are unfairly targeted by certain states or political environments, further fueling their loyalty to Trump as a protector against perceived injustices.

Over the last decade, the declining trust in institutions has opened the floodgates to real-world consequences and was exponentially worsened during the COVID-19 pandemic. Many Trump supporters rejected scientific guidance on masks and vaccines, driven by a belief that government and public health institutions were misleading them. A heightened degree of skepticism undermined efforts to control the pandemic and highlighted the deep erosion of trust in traditional sources of authority.

Similarly, the aftermath of the 2020 presidential election saw the rise of the "Stop the Steal" movement, where claims of voter fraud persisted despite extensive evidence to the contrary.[1] The movement culminated in the January 6th Capitol riot, an event that starkly illustrated how the blurring of fact and fiction can lead to dangerous actions when individuals believe their core values and identities are under threat.

Our book delves into the social science theories that help explain the psychological underpinnings of Trumpism. Chapters explore how cognitive dissonance, moral disengagement, and rationalization allow supporters to reconcile conflicting information and justify their unwavering loyalty.

For instance, one participant in Scottsdale, Arizona, bluntly noted:

> *"You're not going to have [a] 100 percent ethical moral-based man serving as president. It's just ... an impossibility in our world today."*

This rationalization is a common thread among Trump supporters, where the acknowledgment of flaws does not diminish their support but becomes part of its justification. The psychological mechanisms outlined in the pages ahead are not unique to Trump supporters; rather, they are a fundamental aspect of the human condition. What truly sets this unique phenomenon apart is the degree to which his supporters adeptly employ these mechanisms in support of a political figure who consistently challenges the traditional norms of morality, truth, and ethical behavior.

Moreover, we examine the tribalistic "us vs. them" mentality that has become so prevalent in American politics.[2] This is not just a political strategy; it is a social dynamic that plays on a person's deepest fears and insecurities. Trumpism has leveraged this dynamic to create a cohesive and loyal base, one that sees itself as embattled and persecuted by the "other." The noticeable sense of victimhood displayed during the last decade is not merely a rhetorical device but a central theme in the identity of Trump supporters. Some express a belief in pervasive conspiracy theories, as a participant in Pryor, Oklahoma, remarked:

> "Yeah, it's almost like there's a big computer in the sky that controls everybody. And we can't put our fingers on that person [or] thing. But there's something controlling us."

A quote such as this one illustrates how deeply some supporters feel alienated from mainstream narratives, contributing to their reliance on alternative explanations and their loyal support for Trump.

A particularly poignant example of this dynamic is the story of Pamela Hemphill, a Trump supporter who participated in the January 6th Capitol riot and later came to regret her involvement. Hemphill, who was convicted for her actions, realized that she had been misled by Trump and described him as a "cult leader."[3] Her story is a powerful example of how some individuals can escape the autocratic trap and begin to distinguish between fact and fiction. Hemphill's evolution from an ardent supporter to a vocal critic vividly illustrates the moral and psychological complexities involved in breaking free from intense political allegiances. It also underscores the significant pressure from others within the same group who may challenge and disown you for speaking out.

However, a severe and troubling aspect of Trump's persuasion is intertwining reality with fiction. We live in an era of misinformation, where the lines between truth and falsehood have been unwittingly and deliberately obscured. This phenomenon is not just a challenge for journalists and educators but is a fundamental threat to democracy itself. When citizens can no longer distinguish between reality and propaganda, the very foundation of a democratic society is at risk. Despite this, many supporters cling to Trump even as they may sometimes acknowledge his flaws. As one participant in Richfield, Utah, stated:

> *"I don't blindly support him. I understand he's flawed. But he's the best, flawed candidate that we have."*

This statement captures the essence of what we term the *totality of allegiance,* where supporters are willing to overlook stark imperfections, drastic changes in norms, and even criminal conduct because they believe no better alternative exists. However, the 2024 Republican primary had several viable candidates, all of whom have their own imperfections, like every other human being on the earth.

Throughout each focus group discussion, the majority of supporters confidently asserted that all the other presidential candidates owe their existence and current positions to Trump. This reaction was specifically echoed by a young man from Utah County, Utah, and everyone in the room unequivocally agreed.

In the final sections, we turn from analysis to direction, charting the path forward in an era where adherence to falsehoods has become a defining feature of political life. The challenge of distinguishing fact from fiction is not just an intellectual exercise but a moral imperative. We explore the strategies that can help individuals avoid the deceptions of misinformation and the hazards of cognitive bias. We also discuss what it will take to rebuild a political culture grounded in truth and democratic values.

This research endeavor redirects attention from Trump himself to a deeper exploration of the perspectives, reasoning, and motivations of his supporters, which we firmly believe is critical for a more comprehensive understanding. But this book is also being published at a time when America is at a crossroads. The choices we make in the coming years will determine whether we continue down the path of division and distrust or whether we can find a way back to a united, truthful, and democratic society. The stakes could not be higher, and the time to act could not be more urgent.

Through a comprehensive analysis of Trump supporters, their beliefs, and the social and political dynamics that have brought us to this point, this book sheds light on the underlying forces of this phenomenon and the future trajectory of American society. Engaging critically and empathetically with political discourse is crucial for fostering a healthy, informed, and democratic society.

CHAPTER 1

The Research Study

In today's highly polarized political climate, understanding why people support certain leaders requires more than surveys and statistical analysis. To get to the heart of what drives political allegiances, we turned to focus groups—an approach that allows us to hear directly from supporters in a structured and open environment. Our goal was to move beyond surface-level explanations and explore the deeper motivations behind why individuals continue to support Donald Trump, especially in the face of historical controversies and criticisms.

We recruited participants through a snowball sampling method, where initial participants referred others to join the study.[1] This method is often used in research to reach populations that may be harder to access and relies on participants' social networks to gather a broader group. Many participants were recruited by word of mouth, while others were engaged through social media posts. After completing the survey, participants were compensated with a $30.00 Amazon gift card for their time.

We deliberately chose our sample states; it was not random. Utah, with its strong conservative values and deep religious roots, gave us unique insights into how religious beliefs intersect with political support. South Carolina, a key player in Republican primaries, offered a mix of suburban and rural viewpoints with a notable evangelical influence. Oklahoma provided a purely rural sample, where evangelical beliefs also strongly shape political views. Arizona, with its blend of urban and rural areas, provided a spectrum of perspectives that reflected Trump's broader support base. This diversity ensured that our findings are rich and reflected the wide-ranging motivations behind Trump's appeal.

To accomplish this, we designed a study that combined traditional surveys with focus group discussions throughout these strategic states. Across the country, we conducted 14 individual focus groups with a total of 55 participants—an averaging of 4 to 5 participants per session, though the number varied between groups. The total number of participants included 33 men and 22 women, primarily white, though a few minority individuals (Hispanic, Native American) were also represented. In terms of education, household income, and community type (rural, suburban, urban), our sample was reflective of the broader population, providing a well-rounded view of Trump's support base. However, our focus *was not* just on gathering opinions; we were interested in understanding *why* people hold these beliefs and *how* they navigate conflicting information.

THE SETUP AND EXECUTION OF FOCUS GROUPS

Each session was carefully structured to maximize engagement and insight. The discussions revolved around a video and slide presentation featuring facts about the 2020 election claims and Donald Trump's character and leadership traits. These facts were selected through a rigorous vetting process involving undergraduate and graduate student researchers and us as the research professors. We employed tools such as the CRAAP Test[2] and the TRAAP Model[3] to ensure that the information presented was credible and accurate. These methods evaluate the currency, relevance, accuracy, authority, and purpose of the sources used. This is essential in ensuring that discussions are based on reliable information, to avoid the spread of misinformation.

The sessions opened briefly, explaining the focus group structure, followed by the first discussion about participants' support for Trump. We then transitioned to the video and slide deck presentations. After viewing, each participant answered specific questions about the facts and information they had watched and read. For instance, they were asked to rate how familiar they were with the information presented, how valid they thought the information was, and to what extent the information caused them to question their support for Trump receiving the 2024 GOP and general election nomination. These survey responses allowed participants to reflect on their reactions before joining group discussions.

The group discussions were guided by thought-provoking questions aimed at uncovering deeper insights. Participants were encouraged to share their thoughts on the information, discuss what might have caused them to question the reliability or validity of the information, and consider the best arguments or evidence against what they had seen. We, as the researchers, also prompted participants to think critically about their claims by asking, "What evidence exists for the claim you just made?" These discussions were designed to elicit individual and collective reflections on the issues. Once the group discussion concluded, the participants moved on to the next portion of the video and slide deck. This sequence—video/slide deck, individual reflection, and group discussion—continued throughout each session.

At the end of the session, participants completed a more comprehensive survey that captured additional political views, media habits, and civics knowledge. This full survey is included in the book appendix for reference. The combination of quantitative and qualitative methods—structured surveys followed by open discussions—ensured a holistic view of the participants' beliefs, motivations, and reasoning. The research shared in this book solely focuses on the comments, statements, and discussions that occurred during the focus groups..

Lastly, it is also important to note that while some focus group quotes have been adjusted for grammar or clarity to ensure readability, no major content changes were made. We stayed true to the words and messages that were expressed, ensuring that the integrity of the participants' voices remained intact.

NAVIGATING THE COMPLEXITY OF FOCUS GROUPS

Running focus groups on a polarizing figure like Donald Trump presented unique challenges. Moderator neutrality was crucial—we needed to ensure that participants did not feel pressured to respond in a certain way. To maintain this balance, we used non-leading, open-ended questions and avoided steering the conversation in any particular direction. This allowed the participants' voices to emerge authentically, providing insights that would not have been possible through surveys alone.

It was important to ensure that participants felt comfortable expressing their honest views. To address this, we emphasized the anonymity of the discussions and ensured that all data would be kept confidential. We are trained to create a welcoming environment where participants can speak freely. This approach helped us gather more genuine insights. Drawing from ethical guidelines for scholarly research and specifically human subjects research, we ensured that participants were fully informed of their rights and the voluntary nature of their involvement. This foundation of trust was fundamental to fostering open and honest dialogue. Focus groups offer insights that surveys alone cannot capture, particularly when it comes to understanding the deeper motivations behind people's decisions and beliefs. Unlike surveys, which tend to capture broad trends, qualitative research allows for a deeper exploration of why individuals hold views, providing context and nuance that numbers alone cannot offer.[4]

RESEARCH THEMES AND THE CODING PROCESS

During the focus groups, we used an audio recording device to capture participants' verbal comments. We also took notes of emotions, gestures, and non-verbal actions. A research team member operated the recording equipment, ensuring that comments were recorded. The recordings were transcribed post-session, anonymizing participants by assigning numbers to their respective dialogues. Once transcription was complete, the audio recordings were deleted to ensure participants' privacy. The transcripts served as the primary data for analysis.

The research team used thematic coding—a method that helps identify patterns and themes within qualitative data. Once the focus groups were completed, we transcribed the discussions and began the process of coding—identifying recurring themes, patterns, and ideas that emerged across multiple sessions. The process of qualitative text analysis is a powerful tool for systematically organizing large amounts of textual data and uncovering meaningful insights.[5] Coding allowed us to organize the vast amount of data we collected, bringing out the most important insights while making connections to broader social science theories. The research team used a software called MAXQDA, which is a phenomenal tool for sorting and systematically analyzing qualitative data.[6]

Our coding efforts resulted in 4,115 coding segments, representing specific quotes tied to themes and individual data. This large volume of data was meticulously coded by a team of three graduate students and one professor. The team worked through the data for hundreds of hours, often revisiting the coding structure and refining the categories to ensure the final output was both valid and concise. This was an immense task but critical to accurately capturing the nuance and complexity of the participants' responses.

We will discuss these principal theories, concepts, and themes in much more detail in the chapters ahead, but below are a few examples of how they materialize. One of the key theories that emerged through our coding process was cognitive dissonance—a concept in psychology that describes the discomfort people feel when they hold contradictory beliefs.[7] This dissonance appeared frequently in our focus groups, as participants often expressed conflicting thoughts between their recognition of Trump's flaws and their continued support for him.

In Richfield, Utah, a participant fervently defended Trump's policies after acknowledging some concerning aspects, expressing strong support for the president, especially compared to those in his own party:

> *"... As a general rule, [Trump] is more constitutionally grounded than most Republicans."*

This tension between acknowledging flaws and maintaining loyalty is an indication of cognitive dissonance, and our coding coordination allowed us to track how widespread this sentiment was among the participants.

Other codes, such as confirmation bias, captured how participants processed information that aligned with their pre-existing beliefs.[8] For instance, when shown a video affirming the legitimacy of the 2020 election, several participants immediately dismissed the criticism, citing alternative news sources that supported their views. The code for confirmation bias allowed us to identify these moments and connect them to the larger theory of motivated reasoning—the idea that people are more likely to believe information that supports their existing views, even in the face of contradictory evidence.[9]

In addition to these more complex, overlapping codes, we also identified simpler patterns. For example, the code distrust captured widespread skepticism of mainstream institutions—media, government, and academia. One participant from Mesa, Arizona, bluntly stated:

> *"It's hard to trust anybody anymore. That's my thing. I don't know who to trust."*

This sentiment was repeatedly expressed in our discussions. Participants' comments indicate a deep distrust in the media, elected officials, institutions, and even fellow citizens.

BRINGING THE THEORIES TO LIFE

The real power of focus groups lies in their ability to give voice to the theories we study. The coded themes were more than just abstract concepts; they were also evident in the participants' own words. For example, the quote mentioned earlier about a participant acknowledging Trump's flaws but continuing to support him illustrates a type of moral rationalization or disengagement—the process by which people justify unethical behavior by distancing themselves from its consequences.[10] Theories often overlap due to the sheer complexity of human thought and behavior. Similarly, victimhood emerged as a key theme, with participants frequently expressing their feelings that the media and government unfairly targeted Trump and conservatives in general.[11] One individual from St. George, Utah, firmly said:

> *"[Trump] didn't need the money. He's poorer now than when he went in. I think it's very sad how much he's had to battle everyone even to do what he did while he was in there, let alone when he got out. I don't know that this system that we've got will allow him to be elected. They'll figure out a way that he can't be, even though that's what the people want. Because everything I read he's who people want. He should win again. He should have won."*

By systematically coding these conversations, we could connect what people believed and why they believed it. These insights, when connected with social science and behavioral-related theories, help paint a clearer picture of the motivations behind Trump's support. However, conducting focus groups requires a delicate balance. While we aim to gather thoughtful insights into why people think and feel the way they do, we must also be careful not to influence their responses or push them toward a particular conclusion. The strength of this approach lies in its ability to capture the complexity of human thought—the internal conflicts, the emotional loyalties, and the rationalizations that shape political behavior. Through this process, we connected real conversations with broader theories of human behavior, which has allowed us to offer a more robust understanding of Trump's support. When conducted carefully and thoughtfully, focus groups can provide insights that numbers and surveys alone simply cannot. We are eager to share what we heard and learned.

CHAPTER 2

The Trump Phenomenon

Donald J. Trump's rise, presidency, and ongoing influence signify a distinctive political movement in American history. Unlike most politicians, Trump came from the stereotypical worlds of business and entertainment, and reshaped the concept of leadership in modern American politics. Political comebacks are rare, with President Grover Cleveland being the last to achieve one in 1893. However, Trump's attempt to secure the presidency after his 2020 defeat remains a definite possibility.[1]

The Trump phenomenon goes beyond the man himself. It reflects a significant change happening in American political norms, especially within the Republican Party and political institutions in the United States. This movement is part of a global populist wave that thrives on challenging elites, distrusting the media, and promising to restore national dominance. Our focus group study aims to delve deeper into the motivations, emotions, and frustrations of Trump voters, providing insights that differ from other academic and media analyses. By listening to the voices of those who support him, we gain a clearer understanding of why this phenomenon persists and what it reveals about the state of American democracy.

SHIFTS IN POLITICAL NORMS

The Trump phenomenon has upended some long-standing political traditions. His presidency was marked by numerous unprecedented events, which include his two impeachments, his refusal to concede the 2020 election, his alleged instigation of the insurrection at the U.S. Capitol on January 6, 2021, and his social media use that bypassed traditional media outlets to communicate directly with his supporters.[2] These actions pushed the boundaries of presidential power, raising concerns about democratic erosion.[3] Yet for his supporters, these very actions are seen as strengths.

Many view Trump's defiance of political norms not as a flaw but as a necessary challenge to a system they believe has failed them. One focus group participant from Arizona stated:

> "I never watched [the] news until they started covering Trump. And ever since he left, I haven't watched the news. I think Trump made it fun."

This participant spoke about Trump's ability to disrupt traditional politics and reengage with disillusioned voters who normally do not vote or do not feel heard by normal politicians.

This shift reflects a larger cultural realignment within the United States as populist movements gain traction by rejecting established norms. Trump's rise coincides with majority waves globally, from Brexit to the leadership of Viktor Orbán in Hungary and Jair Bolsonaro in Brazil.[4] These leaders, who are similar to Trump, challenge elites, demonize the press, and appeal to nationalistic and anti-immigrant sentiments.

REPUBLICAN PARTY TRANSFORMATION: FROM CONSERVATISM TO POPULISM

From Trump's political rise to the present day, the Republican Party has undergone a significant transformation. The party, once recognized for conservative principles like fiscal responsibility and limited government, underwent a shift in focus under Trump's leadership. This change emphasizes populism, with an increased focus on nationalism, trade protectionism, and immigration. This change has led many traditional conservatives, such as former Congresswoman Liz Cheney and Senator Mitt Romney, to distance themselves from Trump, as they saw his approach as a departure from the Republican Party's values.

However, a significant portion of the Republican base views Trump as the future of the party due to the success of his policies and leadership during his presidency. A focus group participant in South Carolina articulated his support in this way:

> *"I'm not voting for a pastor or the pope.*
> *I'm voting for somebody to get rid of ISIS,*
> *keep my taxes low, fix the supply chain."*

This participant expressed a very practical perspective in which personal morality is kept separate from political performance. This change is in line with the broader trends in populism as conservatism shifts towards a more populist, reactionary form motivated by a desire to regain lost power. This transformation within the Republican Party indicates not only a shift in policy but also in voter identity, as Trump's supporters increasingly embrace populist rhetoric over traditional conservatism.[5]

MEDIA DISTRUST AND MISINFORMATION

A significant theme throughout Trump's rise has been his antagonistic relationship with the media. From labeling the press the "enemy of the people" to branding any negative coverage as "fake news," Trump has consistently undermined trust in mainstream media.[6] This strategy has resonated with his supporters, many of whom have shifted their trust to alternative outlets like Fox News and Newsmax, which reinforced Trump's narrative. In Washington, Utah, a participant noted in a written response that:

"The Deep State is DEEP."

Comments like this one deeply connect to distrust not only in the media but in all traditional sources of authority. The spread of false information through alternative channels has deepened political divides, making it increasingly difficult for voters to distinguish fact from fiction.[7] Misinformation, particularly surrounding the 2020 election, has fueled anger and disillusionment among Trump's base despite the debunking of such claims by courts and investigators.[8]

EMOTIONAL AND IDEOLOGICAL MOTIVATIONS

By engaging directly with Trump supporters, we went beyond surface-level assumptions to explore the deeper emotional and ideological motivations that drive individuals' allegiance to Trump.

Where traditional media coverage often reduces individuals to statistics, our focus groups provided an intimate setting where participants could express their beliefs, concerns, and frustrations. This approach allowed us to capture the complexity of their motivations, often oversimplified in mainstream analyses. Our method revealed why certain themes—such as anti-elitism, nostalgia, and frustration with the political system—resonate so deeply with Trump's devotees.

These conversations revealed not only the depth of support for Trump but also the emotional intensity behind it. Trump supporters are not a monolithic group, and their reasons for loyalty often intertwine personal experiences with broader political and cultural changes. Many participants expressed a yearning for a perceived loss of American identity and a sense of betrayal toward both political parties. We gained a more holistic understanding of why these voters remain committed to Trump, even amid controversies. For example, a recurring theme was a profound sense of nostalgia for a bygone era. Many participants longed for a simpler, more prosperous time in American history—a period they believe Trump can restore. As one participant from Mesa, Arizona, noted:

> "I feel bad for our kids. ... They don't know what an innocent America is."

This statement encapsulates a broader emotional drive in Trump's admirers: a desire to return to an idealized version of America. Trump, for these voters, symbolizes the possibility of reclaiming that lost identity, fueling their loyalty.

Frustration with the political establishment is another key motivator. Participants consistently voiced dissatisfaction with both parties, seeing Trump as an outsider capable of shaking up the system. One participant from Washington, Utah, summarized with this sentiment:

> "I just kind of liked the way he pushed back, and he wasn't afraid of upsetting people."

This anti-establishment reaction aligns with broader populist trends, where voters gravitate toward leaders who challenge elites, and Trump's supporters often directly admire his defiance of norms. It signals authenticity and strength. However, there were moments when supporters acknowledged Trump's behavior but rationalized their continued support. One participant from Scottsdale, Arizona, expressed this complexity:

> "For what it's worth, we as a nation benefited secondarily because of his narcissism."

Supporters justify Trump's actions as necessary for national success, allowing them to maintain their allegiance without confronting their moral conflicts.[9]

SITUATING TRUMPISM IN THE BROADER LITERATURE

The Trump phenomenon has been explored from many different perspectives, and it is important to situate our work within this broader body of literature. These works typically fall into three categories: pro-Trump perspectives, anti-Trump critiques, and academic/neutral studies that seek to understand the movement through empirical analysis and psychological frameworks.

Pro-Trump works present Trump as a disruptive force for good, positioning him as a necessary challenger to a failing political system. Victor Davis Hanson's *The Case for Trump* is one such work, where Hanson argues that Trump's presidency was a corrective measure against entrenched elites and bureaucratic inefficiency.[10] Books like this emphasize Trump's outsider status and celebrate his willingness to upend traditional political norms, often framing his actions as a fight to restore American values.

In contrast, anti-Trump critiques focus on the dangers of Trump's leadership and the long-term effects of his presidency on democratic norms and institutions. Fred C. Trump III's book, *All in the Family: The Trumps and How We Got This Way,* provides a personal, insider view of the Trump family dynamics that highlights the origins of Trump's controversial behavior.[11] Cassidy Hutchinson's work, *Enough,* offers a unique account from inside the Trump White House, detailing Trump's behavior during pivotal moments such as the January 6th Capitol riot.[12] Another significant work, *Confidence Man: The Making of Donald Trump and the Breaking of America*, by Maggie Haberman, provides a comprehensive journalistic account of Trump's rise, examining how he manipulated media and institutions to consolidate power.[13] These works collectively paint Trump as a disruptive and dangerous force in American politics.

A final class of books grounded in academic studies attempts to understand the Trump phenomenon through the lens of the relationship between Trump, his followers, and the attributes of those followers. Steven Hassan's novel, *The Cult of Trump,* delves into the cult-like devotion Trump commands among his followers, analyzing this loyalty through the lens of psychological manipulation.[14] Tom Schaller and Paul Waldman wrote the book *White Rural Rage: The Threat to American Democracy,* which explores how rural America's economic and social frustrations contribute to the rise of Trumpism, emphasizing the role that perceived betrayal by both political parties plays in fueling this movement.[15]

Other studies, like *How Reasonable Americans Could Support Trump: Helping Liberals Understand the MAGAverse*, by Brian Rees, provide arguments for why Trump supporters see him as their champion, highlighting the deep cultural and ideological divides that define the modern political landscape.[16] Russell Moore's, *Losing Our Religion: An Altar Call for Evangelical America,* addresses the decline of evangelical Christianity, driven by younger generations disillusioned by their elders' support for Trump despite his moral failings.[17] John Hibbing wrote *The Securitarian Personality: What Really Motivates Trump's Base and Why It Matters for the Post-Trump Era,* which presents a compelling psychological analysis, arguing that Trump supporters are driven not by authoritarian impulses but by a desire for protection against perceived threats from welfare cheats, religious and ethnic minorities, and people from other countries.[18] This last category of literature is particularly relevant to our study as it also employs a similar methodological approach, combining interviews and surveys of Trump supporters.

Our work is rooted in the academic tradition but sets itself apart by examining the emotional and ideological motivations of Trump's supporters and recognizing the significance of the predicament we are in today. Our goal in this book is to emphasize the complexity and humanity behind the continued loyalty to Trump.

INSIGHTS INTO THE TRUMP PHENOMENON

Our research aims to explore the relationship between Trump and his supporters, delving into the often intricate and multifaceted reasons behind their loyalty. Whether their support is moderate or fervent, these individuals represent a diverse group of Americans with deep emotional and ideological motivations. In contrast to the dismissive labels often assigned to Trump's devotees, such as "deplorables," our focus group sessions revealed a very different picture.[19] We encountered people who, independent of their political allegiances, are the kind of neighbors and citizens who embody the best of American decency and community spirit. We found a vast group of citizens who range from a 70-year-old man caring for his grandchildren and ailing wife, to selfless, religious individuals providing service to their community, and principled law enforcement officers dedicated to fairness all having a shared commitment to family, faith, and country.

The Trump phenomenon transcends the individual and speaks to a larger transformation in the political landscape of the United States. It signals a profound change in how voters engage with politics and in their trust—or lack thereof—in the institutions that govern them. Our research has allowed us to hear firsthand the voices of Trump supporters, offering insights that go beyond superficial stereotypes. By listening deeply, we uncovered the emotional and ideological foundations that drive their continued support. Through this process, a more nuanced and complex picture emerged, revealing the frustrations, hopes, and values that shape their political choices.

In this moment of deep polarization, empathy and listening are critical. It is through understanding—not vilification—that we can begin to bridge the divides that threaten our democracy. Our findings challenge us to look inward: to recognize the shared humanity even among those with whom we may disagree politically, and to consider how easily devotion to a cause can shift into allegiance so total that it erodes the critical thinking needed to sustain a healthy democracy.

CHAPTER 3

Moral Rationalization

A fascinating aspect of the 2024 presidential election is how much attention has been given to former President Trump's personality or style. In a recent *Deseret News* editorial discussing Trump's supporters, Jacob Hess notes that one of the things Trump's supporters like about him is his "brash style."[1] While it is true that some of his supporters indicate that they like his "style," very often his supporters note that they support him *despite* his "personality" or "style." In early August, Senator Lindsey Graham (R-S.C.) noted that the GOP has "a lot of personality problems."[2]

This chapter focuses on moral rationalization, a key factor in the rise of populist leaders. Most individuals like to see themselves in a positive moral light—as a good person. However, that self-concept is threatened when one engages in unethical acts or supports unethical actions or people. Such behavior can cause one to question whether they are, in fact, a good person. However, another way of protecting our self-concept is to rationalize the wrongness of our actions—i.e., our unethical act is not actually bad. Psychologists, criminologists, sociologists, and historians have conducted extensive research on this phenomenon. Each scholar has coined terms such as moral disengagement,[3] ethical neutralization,[4] and ethical fading,[5] but they all involve the same fundamental issue we'll refer to as moral rationalization; It is in a group of mental mistakes called self-deception.[6]

To protect ourselves from cognitive dissonance and the discomfort that comes along with it, we change our thinking about the conflicting ideas. Leon Festinger articulated that cognitive dissonance revolves around the idea that if an individual knows various things that are not psychologically consistent with one another, that individual will try to make them more consistent in different ways.[7] This refers to the motivating theory, which states that our minds prefer to eliminate dissonance. We generally do not realize we are doing it.

Sociologists David Matza and Gresham Sykes studied juvenile delinquency and began the exploration of cognitive dissonance related to moral behavior.[8] They found that teenagers used five different methods, what they called ethical neutralization, to justify their behavior: 1) denying that they were responsible for it, 2) denying that anyone had been hurt by it, 3) blaming the victim for the harm, 4) putting the focus on the imperfections of those accusing them of misconduct, and 5) making appeals to a higher loyalty—they did the misdeed to do good.

The second central line of inquiry into this phenomenon came from psychologist Albert Bandura,[9] who was trying to understand human atrocities during Nazi Germany and other periods. He developed an explanation for such behavior that he referred to as moral disengagement. The concept derives from a more general theory of human behavior known as social cognitive theory.[10] This theory suggests that, as individuals, we develop standards of behavior to guide our actions toward positive outcomes and away from harmful actions. Bandura pointed out that people can deactivate their self-regulatory system through a process called moral disengagement. This means that individuals can disengage from their usual moral standards and principles, allowing them to justify or rationalize behaviors that they would typically consider unethical or immoral. This deactivation permits individuals to act in ways that contradict their standards without feeling the usual guilt or shame. Examples of these moral disengagement techniques include moral justification, palliative comparison, dehumanization, attribution of blame, and euphemistic labeling.

APPLICATION TO THE FOCUS GROUP

Returning to the topic of Trump supporters, it is worth considering why many continue to support him despite disliking his personality or style. This phenomenon persists even when other viable Republican candidates, who shared their policy perspectives, were available as alternatives.

We are particularly interested in how people use the terms "personality" or "style." When asked about "personality," responses typically mention traits like being shy or outgoing, charismatic or introverted, quirky or quiet. When asked about "style," people often refer to things like being trendy, formal, spontaneous, or organized. Notice that these qualities aren't usually tied to moral judgments—they're seen as personal differences rather than indicators of right or wrong.

However, when people are asked what comes to mind when thinking of someone who lies, cheats, disrespects others, or lacks self-control, the response is often "lack of character." So why do some Trump supporters who do disapprove of such behaviors describe them as issues of personality or style rather than character? This is likely a form of moral rationalization. Referring to someone's behavior as a matter of personality avoids more profound ethical implications. Acknowledging that someone has character flaws but supporting them anyway could reflect on one's values. Thus, a person might opt for the less morally charged term "personality" to avoid this discomfort. This form of rationalization is sometimes called the "use of euphemism."

As mentioned earlier, social scientists have identified several forms of what we call moral rationalization. The *Business Ethics Field Guide* (BEFG),[11] building on the work of Denis Ribeaud and Manuel Eisner, outlines twelve distinct techniques of ethical neutralization and moral disengagement, which it refers to as moral rationalizations.[12] We highlight some of these techniques, using examples from focus group discussions where participants responded to negative but factual information about Donald Trump. We additionally provide examples of how Trump has employed these rationalizations. These techniques are particularly effective because they often contain elements of truth, allowing people to use them to ease their conscience.

1. Denial of responsibility: Also referred to as the agentic shift, denial of responsibility means we place responsibility for our actions on someone or something else. Our brain insists we are not accountable for our behavior.

When asked why his administration struggled to provide widespread access to Coronavirus testing, President Trump responded, "I don't take responsibility at all," attributing the challenges to an unspecified "set of circumstances" and "rules, regulations, and specifications from a different time."[13] Several media correspondents have documented many instances where Trump avoided taking accountability.[14] This stands in contrast to President Truman's famous declaration that "the buck stops here."[15]

2. Denial of injury: To feel better about something we did or plan to do, we tell ourselves that no one was (or will be) hurt by our actions—or they will not be hurt very much.

When confronted with the information that the state of New York had found Donald Trump liable for business fraud and ordered him to pay $454 million in restitution, one of our respondents said the following:

> *"It's really persecution going on in New York where they're accusing him of overvaluing his properties to get loans when there's no harm done. No bank has been defaulted on. There's [sic] no victims in this."*

Understanding the pivotal role of trust in facilitating smooth business operations, as well as the detrimental impact of diminishing trust on associated transaction costs and the overall creation of wealth, underscores the substantial harm inherent in this behavior.

3. Denial of the victim: Sometimes referred to as victim blaming, occurs when we want to excuse poor behavior. We use ideas such as "She should have known better" or "He had it coming," to convince ourselves that the wounded party is actually the party at fault—and thus not really our victim at all.

When presented with evidence of Trump's immoral behavior, including his bragging about sexually assaulting women, one of our participants made the following statement:

> *"I thought it was gross, but I didn't think it was a sexual assault because, to me, that's a criminal action. Yeah, and I didn't think that's what he was doing. I thought he was getting by with it because he was a star, and they wanted to be with him and let him do whatever some women will."*

4. Condemning the condemner: We focus on finding fault in the entities or people who might criticize us to combat the criticism we fear because of our actions.

When journalists at the National Association of Black Journalists conference asked Donald Trump why black voters should support him despite his well-documented negative statements about black individuals, he did not address the question. Instead, he attacked the journalist and her network. He stated:

> *"Well, first of all, I don't think I've ever been asked a question in such a horrible manner, first question. You don't even say, 'Hello. How are you?' Are you with ABC? Because I think they're a fake news network, a terrible network, and I think it's disgraceful ..."*[16]

Meanwhile, Trump's supporters have recognized and utilized his tactics. For instance, some participants mentioned concerns with "Trump Derangement Syndrome"—a term used to discredit those who might criticize Trump by suggesting that they have a mental disorder, thus freeing them from having to confront the arguments presented to them. For example, we heard the following comment in one of our focus groups:

> *"So, the other thing is that there is such a mental disorder, literally, for those people who hate Trump. I see it in personal friends, and I know that they will hate him. And it doesn't matter what the issue [is], if he's for it, they hate it. And it's become a real mental problem for the Trump haters. I've never seen anything like it."*

5. Appeal to higher loyalties: Ethical dilemmas often require choosing one value over another. This makes appealing to your higher loyalties a particularly effective neutralization technique.

For many of our participants, Trump's character did not matter as long as they thought he could be a good president. Following are some examples of their comments:

> *"I don't like Trump, but I'm 100% behind Trump. I don't like the way he handles himself with people. I think there's times when he's an arrogant butt, and his delivery is horrible sometimes. But that's not why I'm voting for him to be my president."*

> *"I guess I don't care what kind of a person he is personally. I care what kind of a president he is and his presence in the world."*

> *"You know, there's a kind of a saying, a joke, whatever you want to call it, going around. When Trump got elected the first time ... people were complaining about his morality, complaining about his past actions, complaining about this. And the thing was, if you come home from a vacation and your house is full of rats, I mean, your house is totally overrun with rats when you call the exterminator, do*

> *you care if he goes to church? Do you care if he's religious? Do you care if he's righteous? No. You want someone to get rid of the rats. And that's kind of the way people looked at Trump. He was going to drain the swamp, get rid of the rats, whatever terms you want to put on it. And they really didn't care about his personal life."*

6. Moral ledger: Like "cheat day" on a diet, the moral ledger technique permits you to act less ethically in some domains because of the good you have done in others. It's as if unethical acts can be paid for, on balance, by the ethical choices you've made.

For several of our participants, Trump's ability to do a good job as president, allows them to overlook the negative things he does in his personal life. For example, we heard the following:

> "If he's a bad person, it's okay. He's still going to do good."

> "I don't like the way he conducted his marriage stuff, but that's none of our business—[his] constantly changing spouses.

> "But the other reason I would support Trump is I like his policies. I may not like

his bombastic nature. I may not like his personal immorality years ago. But I'm not marrying him. And it's not what I'm hiring him to do."

7. **Defense of necessity:** Sometimes, there is a compelling reason something has to be done. More often, our brain exaggerates the necessity to help us feel better about what we are about to do.

One of our participants had an interesting perspective on this topic, arguing that to be President of the United States, it is necessary to be a narcissist. Here's the quote:

"Jordan Peterson talks about just being men in general, that you've got to be a monster. You have to raise your boys to be a monster. And then you have to be able to control it. Right. That's what being a man is. You have to be a monster, but he doesn't have to have the capability of being a monster. But then you have to be able to control [it]. You have to learn how to control it. And yeah, [Trump] lacks a lot of control. But in order to do that job, in order to handle the pressure of everything that you've got, that he goes through, all of that, [you] have to be narcissistic. They have to be, you know, self-serving. That's the nature, I think, of the job."

8. Claim of normalcy: This is the "everyone does it" excuse. By noting cultural, national, company-specific, or industry norms, you convince yourself that your course of action is acceptable.

When faced with evidence of falsehoods, fraudulent behavior, or assaults on women by Trump, we often observed the use of rationalization techniques in the following ways:

> *"I don't feel like it's much different than anybody else in Washington. Okay. You know there's lies going every which way in Washington. I think it's the way they do business—to handle politics is through lies. So, you accept it."*

> *"Does he bully people? Yes. Name a politician who doesn't."*

> *"We all hate."*

> *"I just think they're all crazy."*

> *"You could change the name up there of a whole lot of politicians and say the exact same thing."* (Referring to the focus group presentation slide deck listing facts about Trump's record and behaviors.)

9. Claims of relative acceptability: An action is not so bad because someone with a strong reputation has engaged in it, or compared to someone else's action, yours does not seem as bad.

When confronted with evidence of Trump being unfaithful to his wives and sexually assaulting women, several of our participants noted how Martin Luther King Jr. and John F. Kennedy had also acted inappropriately in a sexual manner.

> *"I just I don't care that he was unfaithful to his wives. Show me a president that wasn't."*

Also, when discussing January 6th, one of our participants suggested the following:

> *"Sure. Well, is that like the mostly peaceful protests throughout the mostly peaceful BLM protests?"*

10. Use of euphemisms: This is subtle changes in words used disguise your action's full impact, even from yourself. For example, the word "restructuring" may feel better than the word "firing"; a "breach of safety protocol" may carry less moral weight than a "debilitating accident."

In addition to our earlier example of individuals using the terms "personality" or "style" instead of "character," we heard:

"It was a non-disclosure agreement. It wasn't hush money."

When faced with the fact that Trump had been found liable for sexual assault, many individuals chose to label him as a "womanizer" rather than using terms such as "rapist," "sexual predator," or "perpetrator." This choice of language may reflect a preference for milder, legally acceptable terminology instead of more explicitly addressing the severity of the actions involved.

We want to stress that these techniques are not limited to Trump supporters. The principles apply to everyone to some degree. However, our current focus is understanding how Trump supporters utilize these techniques to deepen their allegiance. It is imperative for individuals to reflect on their own tendencies toward self-deception and rationalization, and to act with integrity and make better decisions.

CHAPTER 4

Tribalism

In today's political landscape, lines are drawn more sharply than ever. We live in an age where people define themselves not only by what they believe but by who they oppose. This sense of belonging to one group while being against another is what drives modern-day tribalism. It permeates conversations, news outlets, and social media feeds, encouraging a binary mindset—us vs. them. Whether conscious of it or not, this tribal mindset reduces our ability to interpret facts objectively, shaping how we see ourselves and others in the world.

Tribalism is deeply embedded in our politics, and it feels as if loyalty to one's political group has overtaken our ability to engage in meaningful debate or listen to differing viewpoints. It is not just that we disagree with others; increasingly, we view others who don't align with our ideology or values as existential threats. The media and social platforms only amplify these divisions, creating echo chambers where we hear the same opinions reinforced over and over. In such an environment, the ability to think critically and impartially assess facts is eroded, replaced by a fierce allegiance to one's in-group. Donald Trump's rhetoric, particularly his use of phrases like "they're out to get us"[1] or "the fake news media,"[2] exemplifies how divisive language can further deepen these tribal instincts, portraying critics and opponents as enemies of the people.

This chapter explores how these dynamics shape political behavior. We explore the historical roots of us vs. them language and how tribalism has evolved in the age of partisan media and social networks. Additionally, we examine the psychological and social mechanisms that reinforce our biases and shape political allegiances. Through focus group quotes, we gain insight into how these forces manifest in everyday political conversations.

THE TRIBAL THEORIES

Henri Tajfel's social identity theory provides a foundational understanding of why group identities, particularly political ones, have become so embedded in modern society. People derive part of their self-concept from the groups they belong to, leading to a natural preference for the in-group and suspicion or hostility toward the out-group. In the realm of politics, this is why many people feel personally attacked when their political party or beliefs are questioned. Political allegiance is more than just an opinion; it is an expression of personal identity. Debates on issues such as immigration, healthcare, or the economy often feel personal due to this important identification. When people adopt a political stance, they are not simply defending a policy; they are affirming who they are and where they belong.[3] This need for belonging propels much of the polarization we witness today, as political discourse often transforms into a struggle for identity.

Morality also plays a crucial role in deepening attachment to the in-group. For many, loyalty to their group is seen as a moral duty, especially when framed as protecting one's community or country from external threats. This moral framing is evident in debates over issues such as immigration, where restrictive policies are often defended as necessary to safeguard the nation from outsiders. Here, immigration becomes not just a policy matter but a moral imperative to preserve the integrity of the in-group.[4] When political loyalty is moralized in this way, compromise becomes difficult, as concessions are not seen as disagreements but as betrayals.

Echo chambers in media and social networks further amplify these dynamics. Social media algorithms create filter bubbles, exposing individuals primarily to information that reinforces their pre-existing beliefs.[5] These echo chambers encourage confirmation bias, where people only seek out information that aligns with their views while dismissing opposing perspectives. This emotional satisfaction is reinforced by belonging to like-minded groups, leading to political tribalism as individuals become more entrenched in their group's beliefs and less willing to engage with differing viewpoints.

The division between "us" and "them" is often intentionally weaponized by leaders, especially autocrats, who seek to create a clear distinction between a virtuous in-group and a dangerous out-group. Political leaders often use fear and urgency to justify extreme measures, painting political opponents as existential threats. For example, when Trump labels the media as "the enemy of the people," it deepens the divide between political factions, eroding trust in democratic institutions and discouraging critical thinking. In times of uncertainty or crisis, divisive rhetoric becomes more potent. Political leaders tap into fears and use conspiratorial language to frame the out-group as working against the people's interests. By appealing to grievance and victimhood, they strengthen emotional bonds with supporters.[6] Rational discourse is replaced with emotional loyalty, prioritizing group solidarity over independent thought, undermining fact-based debate.

On a psychological level, this dynamic is reinforced by the human tendency to seek information supporting pre-existing beliefs. Known as confirmation bias, this tendency means individuals are more likely to accept information that aligns with their group's beliefs and reject anything that challenges them. During the COVID-19 pandemic, for example, partisan media coverage shaped perceptions of the virus. Those exposed to media that downplayed the severity of the pandemic were more likely to believe the risks were exaggerated, reinforcing their group's stance and dismissing opposing views. This selective processing of information reveals how deeply group identity influences political behavior and how individuals engage with facts and evidence.

These concepts and theories provide a basic and informative framework for understanding why tribalism has become such a powerful force in modern politics. Social identity, moral obligation, and psychological biases contribute to today's deep divisions. Political leaders exploit these dynamics, blurring the line between fact and loyalty, making critical thinking more challenging and political compromise less likely. The upcoming sections will explore real-world examples, followed by focus group participants' reflections on tribalism's effects on everyday life.

TRIBALISM IN THE PAST AND TODAY

As mentioned previously, historically, leaders have strategically used us vs. them language to strengthen their power, create a sense of in-group solidarity, and marginalize dissenting voices. This language effectively constructs the framework of a worldview where the in-group is seen as morally superior and perpetually threatened by a corrupt or dangerous out-group. Leaders justify their actions by portraying opponents as existential threats and rallying their base around a common cause.

In Nazi Germany, Hitler mastered the use of this divisive rhetoric to unite his followers against a range of perceived enemies, from political dissidents to communists. His speeches were filled with references to "they" and "them"—groups that were supposedly conspiring to weaken or destroy the German people. Hitler directed his rhetoric at Jewish people and non-Aryan races, as well as anyone he saw as a threat, creating an atmosphere where opposition meant betrayal. This allowed the Nazi regime to suppress political dissent and justify extreme actions in defense of the in-group's supposed purity and strength.[7]

In the mid-20th century, the United States saw a version of us vs. them language during McCarthyism Senator Joseph McCarthy stoked fears of communist infiltration, dividing the country into two factions: loyal Americans and communist sympathizers.[8] His rhetoric was authoritarian in nature, with the relentless portrayal of the out-group as traitors plotting to overthrow the American way of life. McCarthy's speeches and hearings fostered a culture of paranoia, where even mild political dissent was viewed as evidence of subversion. This rhetorical framework by McCarthy created lasting divisions in American society, with supporters adopting his language based on suspicion and fear.

In Hungary, Prime Minister Viktor Orbán has similarly employed us vs. them rhetoric to maintain control and fuel nationalism. Orbán frequently frames external forces—such as the European Union, migrants, and NGOs—as enemies of Hungary, bent on eroding the country's sovereignty and traditional values. His repeated attacks on George Soros, for instance, have painted Soros as a malevolent figure orchestrating Hungary's demise from behind the scenes. This narrative has taken root among Orbán's supporters, who use the same language to express distrust and hostility toward any external influences, mirroring the language of their leader.[9]

In the United States, Donald Trump uses us vs. them rhetoric in ways that connect with these earlier examples. Trump consistently frames his opponents, immigrants, and the media as enemies of the people. His repeated and ranting narrative of a righteous in-group—the "true" Americans—under siege from corrupt elites and dangerous outsiders is consistently on display at his rallies.[10] Trump's ability to stoke these divisions was not just a matter of political expediency; it also demonstrated how effectively a leader's language can be adopted and magnified by their base. Supporters of Trump echo his use of the term "fake news" to discredit any media or information that does not align with their worldview, showing how deeply these us vs. them narratives penetrate public discourse.[11]

A common theme among these examples is the intentional use of "us vs. them" language to identify opponents and bolster group loyalty. But, moving from the leaders directly, we proceed by showing how these elements play out in everyday life and how a leader's supporters feel, believe, and express some of these very ideas that have come from the very top.

EVERYDAY MANIFESTATIONS OF TRIBALISM

The influence of comments and statements from leaders and the media on everyday conversations is remarkable. The language used in these communications becomes ingrained in how individuals perceive the world, whether in its complexity or in black and white. In our focus groups, participants used tribal language and rhetoric as they discussed Trump, particularly statements that were perceived to be against what they stand for. An older female participant from Oklahoma expressed deep concerns about societal institutions, such as schools, feeling they are being influenced by far-left ideologies and promoting incorrect teachings and values. She stated:

> "It's a type of taking over from brainwashing. Because it's which is what's going on in school right now. They are brainwashing our children. The TV shows, the ... the everything is brainwashing, just exactly like the Nazis."

The comment suggests that strong distrust of institutions outside a specific group may be connected to a coordinated effort by certain entities, such as educators, the media, and other societal forces aligned with liberals, Democrats, or the far left, to influence children. The language used in the comment creates an "us vs. them" mentality, portraying the other group as the enemy attempting to undermine the values of the in-group. The reference to Nazis heightens the perceived threat, demonstrating how tribalism can lead to extreme comparisons and the vilification of out-groups.

In another focus group, an older man from St. George, Utah, wanted to make sure everyone knew that there was a nefarious force working to undermine Trump, who represents him and his in-group by stating that:

> "Politicians will do everything they can to keep him from office."

This statement unequivocally demonstrates how tribalism fosters fear and distrust among the in-group by creating a strong sense of opposition from the out-group. It reflects confirmation bias and oversimplifies complex political realities into a battle for survival between opposing factions. The same participant further commented:

> *"That's the problem with politicians, is that they've learned from day one because they've. They've got people there that have grown up in it and go and be pages, and then they're assistants, and then they, they climb their way through, and they are entrenched."*

The word "entrenched" suggests that the participant views political elites as a self-serving group disconnected from the lives of regular citizens. The speaker sees politicians as a distant, uniform group, emphasizing the division between "us" (the regular people) and "them" (the entrenched elites). This lack of trust is reinforced by confirmation bias, as the participant interprets all political actions as evidence of widespread corruption without considering that things are more complex than they appear.

Another participant from Pryor, Oklahoma, distinguished between different kinds of Democrats. In some conversations across our focus groups, Democrats were seen as those who hate America and are driven to destroy the United States. This participant stated:

> *"There are two kinds of Democrats. There's one that is a Democrat of tradition because grandma and grandpa were Democrats, and I'm not afraid of those people. But there are also Democrats that are Democrats because of conviction, and they're the ones I fear because ... They're anti-everything I hold dear. They're the ones that I fear getting in power and leading our country."*

His straightforward comment provides a clear example of how tribalism operates on different levels. The person makes a distinction between "acceptable" Democrats, whom he sees as harmless, and "conviction" Democrats, who are considered a direct threat to their in-group's values. This division shows how partisan identity can become deeply connected to personal values, making political disagreements feel existential.

In Washington, Utah, a female participant reflected on the scrutiny faced by Trump after the 2020 election, firmly saying:

> *"[Trump] obviously isn't the only one that's denied election results. But it seemed like it was they had already planned to vilify him for that, like he was already targeted and made to seem so much worse for questioning it versus other people that are in that on their end maybe had done*

the same thing. And for me, it's the not being able to ask questions that raises red flags. Well, like, why can't we ask questions? Why can't we look into this? Why can't we, you know, and they did you know, they did a lot of investigations ... But the fact that they seemed so targeted at wanting to villainize him and ... sort of villainize anyone that even wanted to ask about it, was, for me, frustrating ... I think, too, that they wear us out. They wear us down with trivia so we don't get into it."

Her comment illustrates motivated reasoning. She rationalizes Trump's denial of the election by arguing that other political figures have done similar things but faced different consequences. The participant perceives a coordinated effort by "they" to unfairly vilify Trump, reinforcing the idea that the out-group is actively working against the in-group. This framing touches on confirmation bias, as the inability to question the election results is seen as proof of wrongdoing, further solidifying the participant's belief that "they" are suppressing the truth.

Lastly, a Scottsdale, Arizona, participant stated defensively on behalf of Trump when talking about authority figures who speak out against Trump, whether in the Republican party or outside of the party.

"They are mostly adversarial to Trump. Not supporters."

Even a short quote such as this one relies on the us vs. them mentality, dividing people into "us" (supporters) and "them" (adversaries). Criticism of Trump, even from within the Republican Party, is dismissed without considering its merits, reflecting confirmation bias.

This chapter underscores the importance of understanding how tribalism and the us vs. them rhetoric intersect to shape political thought and behavior. The adoption of divisive language from leaders and media figures by everyday citizens reveals the determined influence of these narratives on public discourse. When political identities become intertwined with personal values and worldviews, the line between fact and fiction blurs further, and loyalty to the in-group takes precedence over critical thinking. By examining the voices of the focus group participants, we gain a deeper understanding of how these dynamics play out in real life and why breaking out of these entrenched divisions is so difficult. In the end, this exploration matters because it shows how the very foundation of democratic discourse—reasoned debate, compromise, and mutual respect—is at risk when tribalism takes deep root.

CHAPTER 5

Victimhood

Victimhood is a concept as ancient as civilization itself, yet its role in modern political discourse has gained renewed prominence. Throughout history, leaders have harnessed feelings of grievance and victimization to rally their base, often with far-reaching consequences. A political party that uses victimization for persuasion and moving the masses does not choose the victim arbitrarily.[1] A foundational element in our focus group discussions revolved around the belief that Trump and each of them are facing adversaries from all fronts, both within and outside the established system. This feeling and sentiment has been expressed clearly by

Trump throughout elections as well as in his business ventures, and his supporters identify and connect with his bold declarations. Understanding this narrative of victimhood is critical not only for analyzing politics but also for grasping how it informs identity, loyalty, and action among Trump's devoted followers.

VICTIMHOOD'S POWER

Jason Stanley articulates superbly in *How Fascism Works* that fascist movements manipulate narratives of victimhood to gain and consolidate power by presenting their supporters as under siege from malevolent external forces.[2] Stanley's insights offer a valuable lens to examine the persistent loyalty of Donald Trump's supporters, many of whom perceive themselves as victims of a political and social system that has systematically marginalized their voices. However, the relationship between victimhood and the Trump phenomenon is more nuanced than it first appears. While his supporters often express feelings of victimization—believing that they have been left behind by globalization, cultural shifts, and an unresponsive political establishment—they intensely resist applying the label of "victim" to Trump himself. Even though he is viewed as being persecuted, that label shows weakness. But, clearly, a deep connection to this victimhood theory exists with his followers.

One case in particular tackles this exact situation. During a Utah County, Utah, focus group, we started a conversation about how Trump is portrayed and treated by the media, the Democrats, those who are against him, and institutions such as the U.S. Justice System. We questioned everyone in the group whether Trump could be labeled as a victim because he is being bullied, negatively covered, or unfairly attacked. An older female participant reacted quickly:

> *"He's totally not a victim."*

Without hesitation, she continued to defend Trump and states:

> *"Well, he gets attacked, he gets attacked constantly and he stands up and he fights back. That's not a victim. And so he fights back against everything, and he'll fight back against the fact that he perceived election fraud. He fought back because he is constantly. If you want to see someone who's bullied, it's Trump. He's not a victim, though. He stands up and he doesn't take it."*

Many similar to this participant describe him as a figure who is persecuted or unfairly attacked, but there is a distinction that underscores their perception of strength and resistance in the face of adversity. To his supporters, Trump is a fighter and fights for them against the deep state, the media, and the establishment both inside and outside the Republican Party.

The idea of victimhood has been widely studied in relation to populism and identity politics. Political scientists and psychologists have observed how perceptions of being victimized can unite groups, creating a sense of solidarity within the group and leading to hostility towards perceived outsiders. This is a significant aspect of Trump's rhetoric during rallies and speeches, where he depicts himself not only as a victim, but also as part of a larger conspiracy in which his supporters are also victims.[3] Fascist regimes, for example, often manipulate narratives of victimhood to create a sense of existential threat among supporters. Stanley states that any perceived threat is framed as an attack on the group's identity, values, or way of life, making the defense of these elements a moral imperative.[4]

Collective victimhood is particularly potent in populist movements, when leaders position themselves as defenders of the people against corrupt elites and a broken political system, typically caused by the government. Collective victimhood operates within a political group. When a group perceives itself as a victim of systemic injustice, this perception can form the basis of a shared identity, which activates collective action.[5] For Trump supporters, the sense of victimhood is tied to various grievances: economic dislocation due to globalization, cultural alienation from shifting societal norms, and a feeling of disenfranchisement within the political system. These grievances are often amplified by Trump's rhetoric, which echoes the frustrations of his base and positions him as their champion against an unjust establishment.[6]

Psychologist Vamik Volkan explored the psychological dimensions of victimhood, emphasizing how leaders can manipulate these feelings to maintain power. Volkan suggests that people who identify as victims are more likely to support authoritarian leaders who promise to restore their lost status and protect them from external threats.[7] Trump's campaign slogan, "Make America Great Again," deeply resonates with supporters who feel that their country has been taken from them. This narrative not only validates their sense of loss but also provides a blueprint for reclaiming what they believe is rightfully theirs and has been weakened and attacked.

A participant from Washington, Utah, articulated this sense of embattlement, describing how Trump's steadfastness in the face of relentless attacks by the media and political establishment earned her respect:

> *"I think my respect for Trump began years ago when he did not concede to what the media was trying to put into his mouth or to the appearance. They want to give him a different appearance, and he stood firm for what he was. [He] didn't acquiesce to what the media wanted to say or put in his mouth, and I liked him because the*

media hated him. The Democrats hated him, the Socialists hated him. Half of the Republican Party hated him. And I thought he must have done something either really horrible or really good to have that many people attacking him."

This perception of victimhood is not just passive—it is valorized. Trump's refusal to yield to pressure is viewed as a display of strength, a quality that his supporters admire and aspire to emulate, even though his assertiveness and tendency to fight back often contradict the values and norms they are taught. Victimhood is converted from a mark of weakness into a badge of honor, symbolizing resistance against overwhelming odds.

THE ROLE OF THE MEDIA

The role of media in cultivating and reinforcing the narrative of victimhood among Trump supporters cannot be overstated. Right-wing media outlets, including Fox News and Newsmax, consistently present news stories that emphasize the idea that conservatives, and particularly Trump supporters, are being unfairly targeted by powerful elites. Whether it is the portrayal of Trump's legal challenges, the investigation into Russian interference in the 2016 election, or the aftermath of the January 6th Capitol riot, right-wing media frames these events as part of a broader conspiracy to undermine Trump and his supporters.[8]

A older male from South Carolina captured this dynamic and media framing by firmly stating:

> "Keep going after Trump. Knock yourself out. You're not going to win."

This defiant attitude reflects the influence of media narratives portraying Trump and his supporters as embattled yet resilient, fighting against an overwhelming tide of hostility and deception. The relationship between media and victimhood in populist movements has historical precedents.

During the rise of fascism in Europe, leaders like Hitler and Mussolini skillfully used propaganda to portray their movements as the true representatives of the people, encircled by corrupt elites and foreign enemies.[9] This narrative was essential in consolidating their power and justifying increasingly authoritarian measures. Similarly, in contemporary America, the media's role in shaping the Trump movement's sense of victimhood has been central in maintaining his base's loyalty and justifying his more extreme actions. The narrative of victimhood is not merely a reflection of genuine grievances but also a political tool. By convincing his supporters that they are under constant attack, Trump and his allies can galvanize and mobilize a deeply loyal and highly motivated base. This manipulation of fear and nostalgia helps to maintain

Trump's political power, even as it entrenches a sense of victimhood among his supporters. As a participant from Pryor, Oklahoma, noted:

> *"... They're trying their best to take that man down, and they probably will succeed because I don't think he has a chance of winning this time around."*

A profound fatalism pervades much of the Trump base—a belief that the system is so rigged against them that their efforts, while self-sacrificing, may ultimately be in vain. Yet this belief does not lead to disengagement; instead, it fuels a defiant resolve to fight back, even if the odds are stacked against them. This dynamic mirrors historical examples where leaders used narratives of being under siege to justify extraordinary measures.

VICTIMHOOD IN HISTORY

The politics of victimhood have been a recurring theme in various authoritarian and populist movements. For instance, during the Weimar Republic, Adolf Hitler and the Nazi Party used narratives of German victimhood to rally support after the humiliation of World War I and the Treaty of Versailles.[10] In the American context, the narrative of victimhood has shaped political movements from the Civil Rights era to the present day. In recent years, right-wing populist movements have flipped the script of victimhood, portraying white Christian conservatives as the true victims of a liberal, multicultural elite.[11] This narrative reflects broader cultural and demographic shifts that have unsettled certain segments of the population, leading to feelings of alienation and displacement.

Similarly, far-right movements across Europe today have used victimhood narratives to justify their stance against immigration, globalization, and liberal elites.[12] Victimhood's narrative also possesses a moral dimension, complicating the political landscape further. When individuals or groups see themselves as victims, they often believe they are morally justified in their actions, no matter how extreme. This can lead to an escalation in rhetoric and behavior, as the perceived moral high ground can provide an opening for stricter policies and tactics. The belief in Trump's moral righteousness is reminiscent of authoritarian movements, where leaders positioned themselves as the last bastion of moral virtue against corrupt and evil forces. This moral framing helps explain why Trump's supporters are willing to overlook his flaws—because, in their view, his cause is just, and his enemies are both numerous and unscrupulous.

Our exploration of victimhood in the Trump movement reveals the existence of a deeply intertwined relationship between personal identity, political allegiance, and media influence. Trump supporters, by positioning themselves as victims, have forged an identity that fuels their political engagement. This identity is then shaped by a media ecosystem that continually reinforces their sense of grievance and a political leader who leverages these feelings to maintain his influence.

CONSEQUENCES OF THE VICTIMHOOD NARRATIVE

The political and social consequences of the victimhood narrative are enormous. Fostering a sense of siege and alienation deepens polarization and erodes the foundations of democratic norms. When people believe they are fighting for their own survival, extreme measures can become defensible in their minds, leading to an escalation in rhetoric and, in some cases, violence. This dynamic was tragically evident on January 6th, when a mob of Trump supporters stormed the U.S. Capitol, convinced that they were defending their country from a stolen election.[13] Victimhood fused with lies is a grave danger when people do not recognize the reality of the wrongs and the rights.

And this sense of victimhood can worsen and compound as lies fester. A participant from Mesa, Arizona, expressed the ongoing frustration many Trump supporters feel about being under siege:

> *"About January 6th. It kills me. They're still out there arresting people a year later. Yet the people that burned Oregon, Washington, nothing. So that to me is BS."*

Comments such as these were common. They underscore the deeply ingrained belief that Trump supporters are being persecuted while others are not held to the same standard. The perception of a "two-tiered system" of justice has become central to Trumpism's victimhood, further entrenching the sense of alienation and resentment that fuels the movement.

The belief in victimhood expressed by Trump and his supporters is not just a political strategy; it's an emotional bond rooted in nostalgia, fear, and the belief that they are fighting for America's soul. This sense of moral righteousness, combined with the perception of being under attack, makes the Trump movement more than just a passing political trend. Understanding the role of victimhood in shaping political behavior will be crucial for anyone seeking to bridge the deep divisions in American society. Addressing the roots of perceived victimhood could be the key to healing the fractures in the American political landscape.

CHAPTER 6

Conmen, Cults, and Those Who Follow

The relationship between charismatic leaders and their followers is not rooted in ignorance but in deeper, more complex human needs: belonging, certainty, and trust. In this chapter, we explore how conmen and cult-like figures, particularly in the political sphere, exploit these needs to foster an allegiance that erodes critical thinking. By examining historical and contemporary examples, we uncover the psychological mechanisms that allow such figures to thrive—even in the face of deception. Charismatic leaders possess a unique ability to offer promises of economic stability, social identity, and moral clarity. These leaders and manipulators do not thrive because their followers are naïve but because of the universal human need for belonging and certainty in times of uncertainty. By manipulating these needs, charismatic leaders foster deep emotional attachments, creating a bond so strong that it persists even when followers are presented with contradictory information.

THEORIES ON CONMEN AND CULT-LIKE BEHAVIOR

The term "conman" dates back to the mid-19th century and originates with William Thompson, a New York-based criminal who used a seemingly simple but effective tactic: he would approach well-dressed passersby, strike up a conversation, and ask, "Have you confidence in me to lend me your watch until tomorrow?" Astonishingly, many people handed over their valuables, and Thompson would disappear, leaving the victim to wonder how they had been deceived so easily. This gave rise to the term "confidence man" or *conman*—a person who exploits trust to manipulate others.[1] In his 1857 novel, *The Confidence Man: His Masquerade*, Herman Melville further explores the concept of the conman. Melville sheds light on the psychological and social tactics used by conmen to trap their victims. He portrays his conman as a skilled deceiver who exploits people's trust and vulnerabilities for personal gain.[2] This notion of confidence as both a psychological tool and a weapon underscores the techniques used by historical and modern-day conmen alike. In her book *The Confidence Game*, Maria Konnikova outlines the steps conmen use to manipulate their victims, starting with the "put-up," where the conman identifies the ideal victim, or "mark." The con then progresses through the stages of building rapport and emotional investment before reaching the "blow-off," where the victim is left with nothing.[3] The key to manipulation is creating a personal connection, making the victim feel part of something exclusive and meaningful. This emotional investment is critical for maintaining control over the victim, leaving them vulnerable to further deception.

THE PSYCHOLOGICAL AND SOCIAL MECHANISMS OF THE CON

At the core of every con is the ability to exploit the universal human need for trust and belonging. Conmen do not rely solely on the naiveté or ignorance of their victims but on the victims' desire to believe in something or someone larger than themselves—whether it's financial security, social identity, or moral certainty. As Melville illustrates, the act of gaining confidence is more than a matter of trickery; it is an exploitation of human psychology, where emotions often override critical thinking.[4]

The mechanisms employed by conmen are not dissimilar from the tactics used by cult-like leaders or charismatic figures in politics. These individuals create a narrative that taps into the hopes, fears, and insecurities of their audience, offering a grand vision that feels too important or promising to ignore. This manipulation of trust and belonging forms the foundation of both financial cons and political schemes, creating a deeply emotional allegiance that is difficult to sever—even when evidence of deception comes to light.[5]

The historical examples of Charles Ponzi and Bernie Madoff further demonstrate how conmen, by mastering the art of trust-building, can lure even the most rational individuals into their schemes. Charles Ponzi's notorious scheme in the early 20th century is one of the most well-known examples of this manipulation. Ponzi promised incredible returns on investments, and his charm, combined with the illusion of success, allowed him to gain the trust of thousands.[6] Despite mounting evidence of fraud, his investors remained loyal, caught in the emotional lure of wealth and stability that Ponzi seemed to provide.

Bernie Madoff's scheming included systematic fraudulent behavior. Madoff defrauded thousands of investors and followed a similar pattern. By cultivating an image of trust and expertise, Madoff attracted individuals seeking financial security. Even when cracks in his empire began to show, many continued to believe in the myth he had constructed, unwilling to confront the reality of their losses.[7] His ability to manipulate emotions and build false trust echoes the tactics of political conmen who promise security and prosperity in exchange for unquestioning allegiance.

CHARISMATIC AUTHORITY WITH DARKNESS

The techniques used by Ponzi and Madoff are not confined to the world of financial fraud. Political conmen employ similar strategies, not offering promises of wealth, but of national security, social identity, and a return to perceived greatness. These leaders rely on the same fundamental emotional drivers—trust, belonging, and fear—to build loyalty and devotion.

One of the key psychological mechanisms that explains why individuals remain loyal to charismatic leaders—even in the face of contradictory evidence—is cognitive dissonance. When followers are confronted with information that conflicts with their deeply held beliefs, they experience discomfort and must resolve this dissonance. People often reframe information to preserve their worldview, especially when they have invested emotionally, socially, or financially in a particular leader.[8]

The concept of charismatic authority further explains the depth of these emotional bonds. Charismatic leaders, like many historical conmen, derive their power not from established institutions or principles but from personal magnetism and a sense of exceptionalism. Followers of these leaders feel they are part of a larger mission, often believing that only their leader can solve the issues facing society.[9]

The Mere Exposure Effect, described by Robert Zajonc in 1968, offers additional insight into how followers become more attached to charismatic figures through repeated exposure to their public appearances, speeches, or media presence. Zajonc's research demonstrated that the more often individuals are exposed to a stimulus, the more positively they tend to respond to it—even in the absence of rational justification.[10] This phenomenon aligns with how followers grow more committed to political conmen through constant exposure to their messages, regardless of the content or veracity of those messages.

However, the tactics of conmen and cult-like leaders go beyond simple manipulation. Many of these figures exhibit traits from the Dark Triad of Personality, a psychological model that encompasses narcissism, Machiavellianism, and psychopathy. As Paulhus and Williams describe in their study, these traits are often found in individuals who manipulate others for personal gain.[11]

1. Narcissism: A trait characterized by grandiosity, self-admiration, and a need for validation. Leaders with narcissistic traits, such as Donald Trump, portray themselves as exceptional and deserving of admiration and loyalty, creating narratives that center on their personal success and competence, drawing in followers by appealing to their desire to associate with success.

2. Machiavellianism: A personality trait where individuals are strategic, cunning, and manipulative. They focus on the endgame rather than ethical considerations. Many conmen and cult leaders display Machiavellian traits by strategically manipulating information, creating false narratives, and exploiting others to achieve their goals. An example of Machiavellian manipulation is how Trump handles information and misinformation, presenting himself as the only person capable of "saving" the nation, regardless of the truth.

3. Psychopathy: People with psychopathic traits lack empathy, are remorseless, and tend to behave antisocially. They can be charming and gain others' trust while remaining emotionally detached from their actions. This makes them dangerous, especially in positions of power.

The presence of these Dark Triad traits in political leaders is not uncommon. These three traits enable individuals to rise to power by giving them an advantage over more ethical individuals.[12] Steven Hassan's BITE Model (Behavior, Information, Thought, and Emotional Control) further illuminates the tactics cult-like leaders use to control their followers. Leaders maintain control by manipulating behaviors, controlling information, shaping thoughts, and exploiting emotions. Followers are often isolated from opposing viewpoints and exposed only to narratives that reinforce the leader's authority.[13]

PENNY SWAN'S STORY: BREAKING FREE FROM MANIPULATION

A former Trump evangelist, Penny Swan, provides a striking example of resolving cognitive dissonance and breaking loyalty to a conman or cult-like leader. Swan, a politically active Republican from Hillsdale, Michigan, had long advocated for Trump and his policies. Deeply embedded in her local Republican Party chapter, she was not only a supporter but also a key figure within the MAGA movement. She believed in Trump's narrative of restoring America to greatness. She felt loyal within her political circle, but cracks appeared after the 2020 election. Swan, who had once been an enthusiastic participant in the local Trump-aligned faction, started to watch fellow Trump supporters' behavior shift toward extremism. The party's infighting and radicalization, which included harassment and purges of members who were not loyal enough to the MAGA cause, led her to question her involvement.[14]

Swan's allegiance reached its peak as she watched the January 6th insurrection from afar, unable to participate due to health concerns. Initially, she supported the movement's efforts to challenge the election results, but the violent actions at the Capitol and the increasingly divisive rhetoric among her local group made her reconsider her position. She slowly distanced herself from Trump and his supporters and started to criticize the movement she had once been a part of. This shift was not easy. As Swan distanced herself from the far-right extremism that had taken over her local Republican chapter, she encountered not only harassment but also threats from former allies who now saw her as a traitor. The break was not just political—it was deeply personal. Her experience demonstrates how people can break free from extreme movements when the psychological discomfort becomes too excessive to ignore, and they start prioritizing their personal integrity over group loyalty.[15]

PARTICIPANT INSIGHTS: LOYALTY, IDENTITY, AND RATIONALIZATION

The focus group quotes in the next few pages reveal the complex emotional dynamics underlying loyalty to charismatic leaders like Donald Trump. Supporters form a deep emotional connection to the narrative he has created, portraying himself as a defender of the everyday American against internal and external threats. He is also viewed as an extraordinary fighter for the everyday American who needs protection from his enemies who are ceaselessly attacking him. This narrative is best portrayed by a Pryor, Oklahoma, participant, who stated:

> *"We've never had another president that allowed a group of Christians to come in and pray over him in the Oval Office. [He] is the only one that's ever done that. That speaks volumes to me. This is also*

> *the only one that's never taken a salary for being in the office. And look at all the crap he put up with to not get paid for it. That says a lot too. He's in it for the right reasons. He genuinely wants to help this country do better."*

This quote highlights how Trump's supporters often perceive him as a unique leader with strong moral values. This belief is reinforced by the narrative that Trump is exceptional, different from previous presidents, and driven by a genuine desire to improve the country. Cognitive dissonance plays a key role here: despite factual contradictions (e.g., Trump being the third president to donate his salary, after John F. Kennedy and Herbert Hoover), the participant reframes these facts to maintain their belief in Trump's authenticity and righteousness.[16] The reference to prayer in the Oval Office reinforces the idea that Trump's leadership is not only political but also spiritual, further cementing his charismatic authority.

A focus group participant expressed his belief in Trump's convincing narrative of success when he said:

> *"I believe as a negotiator through [Trump's] business background, he has effectively been able to communicate and demand that which is right for America."*

This quote shows how Trump's business persona blends with his political leadership. It reflects the influence of Machiavellian traits, where manipulation and strategic thinking are seen as desirable qualities in a leader. Trump reinforces his followers' emotional allegiance by appealing to the desire for strength and success even though Trump has struggled in businesses with bankruptcies and failed ventures.[17]

Another Pryor, Oklahoma, participant, when asked about the January 6th insurrection, responded:

> *"After the January 6th deal ... I wasn't too good with that. But then after I saw what they were doing to [Trump] ... they are trying their best to take that man down."*

In this example, we observe cognitive dissonance in action. The participant initially expresses discomfort with the events of January 6th, then ultimately reinterprets the situation as evidence of Trump being a victim of persecution. This reinterpretation enables the participant to resolve the internal conflict by shifting blame away from Trump and onto external forces that are supposedly unfairly targeting him. This sentiment aligns with Steven Hassan's BITE model, where control over the narrative reinforces group loyalty and isolation from alternate viewpoints.[18]

Fear is commonly used by leaders to control their followers. They create a story where it is "us vs. them," making the followers feel constantly threatened by external forces. This makes their followers more emotionally invested in the leader's cause which reinforces group loyalty and unifies followers with a shared sense of mission. One focus group participant from Scottsdale, Arizona, expressed this fear directly:

> *"Voting ID and the scare of, you know, illegal immigrants being able to vote ... I'm more inclined to say there is voter fraud in that case, you know, between, like, mail-in ballots and illegal immigrants."*

By instilling this fear, Trump has been able to maintain a loyal base, notably as the narrative frames him as the last defense against these perceived threats.

Leaders use dramatic events to distract followers and create emotional bonds while minimizing critical engagement with their policies. For Trump, rallies became central to maintaining his base. A St. George, Utah, participant remarked:

> *"When he's up in front of people, he's putting on a show, and some of his constituents like that."*

This comment highlights how Trump's leadership often relies on entertainment value to distract from actual policy, failures, or controversies. His supporters connect with him emotionally through the spectacle, which makes them more likely to remain loyal, even when faced with contradictory evidence. Emotional manipulation is a vital tool for cult leaders, who use these highs to foster dependence on the leader's narrative.[19] By entertaining and energizing followers, leaders like Trump create an atmosphere where critical thinking is sidelined in favor of emotional engagement. Rallies and public displays also function as rituals that reinforce group identity. Repeated exposure to a leader, particularly in high-energy environments, increases followers' attachment and trust.[20] This creates an emotional loop in which followers remain loyal despite evidence of deception or failure, driven by the sense of community and spectacle.

THE CULT OF ALLEGIANCE

The focus group quotes illustrate the intricate psychological and emotional components that underpin unwavering loyalty to charismatic leaders. Followers rationalize contradictions and distortions through cognitive dissonance, reframing, and an emotional bond with an extraordinary figure. This allegiance is not just due to ignorance or a lack of critical thinking; it's the result of a strong emotional and psychological investment. Supporters of influential leaders often develop a strong commitment to their leaders, which can sometimes make it challenging for them to assess their actions critically. This can be influenced by the leader's charisma, victim mentality, or perceived moral superiority. The persuasive tactics, emotional influence, and charismatic appeal can make it difficult for followers to reconsider their allegiance. When personal identity becomes closely linked with the leader, followers may not easily recognize deception and may defend their beliefs even when presented with evidence to the contrary.

CHAPTER 7

Authoritarianism and the Strongman

The allure of strongmen and the desire for authoritarian leadership are recurring themes throughout history. In times of social upheaval, economic instability, or perceived threats to national identity, people often gravitate toward figures who promise to restore order and greatness, often at the expense of democratic norms and individual freedoms. This chapter explores historical and contemporary examples to illustrate how this phenomenon manifests and how it has set the stage for authoritarian and totalitarian regimes.

A striking example is Hitler's rise in Germany. Preceding the acceleration and establishment of Nazi Germany and its horrors, the Weimar Republic regime oversaw a dark period of crushing inflation and large-scale fears among the German people. The Weimar Republic was heavily marked by economic hardship and national humiliation post-World War I, and this vulnerability and economic, social, and political insecurities provided an environment for Hitler's ascent to power. Hitler's promise to revive the economy and restore national pride resonated with a population desperate for stability.[1] In *The Origins of Totalitarianism*, Hannah Arendt explains that totalitarian movements thrive in environments where traditional social structures are crumbling and people are searching for clear, simple solutions to complex problems.[2] Hitler capitalized on the turmoil in society and his compelling leadership skills to win over the German population, particularly due to his sensational narcissism, charismatic talent, and profound desire for power. Arendt provides a specific context for the rise of authoritarian leaders, detailing how they gain favor through lies, deceit, and propaganda. In one of her most convincing quotes, she states:

> *"Before mass leaders seize the power to fit reality to their lies, their propaganda is marked by its extreme contempt for*

facts as such, for in their opinion fact depends entirely on the power of man who can fabricate it."

Authoritarians and leaders in these environments cleverly motivate people with partisan propaganda, creating a strong anti-fact brigade that challenges truth in citizens' minds. Arendt continues in her seminal work, stating, "A mixture of gullibility and cynicism is prevalent in all ranks of totalitarian movements, and the higher the rank, the more cynicism weighs down gullibility."[3] Arendt's quote highlights the significant cynicism of leaders and how they may not honestly believe in the ideologies and propaganda they promote. Instead, they are willing to use manipulation, falsehoods, and lies to control and influence the masses, even though they are fully aware of their deceit. Additionally, followers' gullibility presents a particular challenge, as they are more likely to accept false narratives over truth due to limited access to accurate information or feeling overwhelmed by the abundance of information available. This leaves them susceptible to believing in charismatic authority. Strong leaders take advantage of their followers' naivety while staying emotionally detached. However, followers, even when being deceived, may feel skeptical and distrust mainstream media or intellectual elites. Cynicism can seep in when they become disillusioned by traditional institutions but still hold on to their leader's narrative.

Similarly, Stalin's rise in the Soviet Union followed the chaos after the Russian Revolution. Civil war and famine overshadowed the Bolshevik Revolution's initial promises of equality. Stalin capitalized on this disillusionment, positioning himself as the leader who could restore order and guide the nation toward a brighter future.[4] Like Hitler, Stalin used propaganda, purges, and a cult of personality to solidify his control and suppress dissent, creating a totalitarian state.[5] These historical examples demonstrate how societal instability combined with charismatic leadership can erode democratic institutions and open the door to authoritarian regimes. This dynamic continues in contemporary politics.

In recent years, we have seen the resurgence of authoritarianism with leaders like Viktor Orbán in Hungary, Recep Tayyip Erdoğan in Turkey, and Jair Bolsonaro in Brazil or, to an even more severe degree, Kim Jong Un in North Korea. These leaders emphasize national sovereignty, law, and order and often reject traditional liberal democratic norms.[6] They portray themselves as the only ones capable of defending their nations against internal and external threats, appealing to voters' fears and desires for security.[7] The ascension of Donald Trump to the position of President of the United States stands as a contemporary and notable example of the attraction of a strong, authoritative figure in a democratic framework who exhibits authoritarian characteristics. Trump's rhetoric is centered on themes of restoring American greatness and securing borders, often undermining established political norms, the media, and the judicial system.[8] His ability to cultivate a fiercely loyal base willing to overlook or embrace his authoritarian tendencies highlights the appeal of strongman figures in times of perceived crisis.

There is a human tendency for people to rely less on self-governance and more on finding a strong leader who can guide them through life. This philosophical insight is reflected in past and modern politics, where a strongman's appeal is rooted in a desire for simplicity and certainty in an increasingly complex and uncertain world. Strongmen promise to cut through the confusion and restore order, often by any means necessary.[9] This promise especially appeals to those who feel victims of globalization, rapid social changes, or economic turmoil.[10]

In the 19th century, Alexis de Tocqueville penned his renowned work "Democracy in America," in which he astutely anticipated the potential threat of democratic societies succumbing to paternalistic despotism and a tyrannical individual with complete and unchecked power. Tocqueville cautioned that citizens, grappling with the complexities of self-governance, could be inclined to turn to a powerful central authority for relief, ultimately paving the way for the emergence of soft despotism and tyranny. He writes:

"I see an innumerable crowd of like and equal men who revolve on themselves

> *without repose, procuring the small and vulgar pleasures with which they fill their souls. Above this race of men stands an immense and tutelary power, which takes upon itself alone to secure their gratifications and to watch over their fate. That power is absolute, minute, regular, provident, and mild. It would be like the authority of a parent if, like that authority, its object was to prepare men for manhood; but it seeks, on the contrary, to keep them in perpetual childhood: it is well content that the people should rejoice, provided they think of nothing but rejoicing. For their happiness such a government willingly labors, but it chooses to be the sole agent and the only arbiter of that happiness; it provides for their security, foresees and supplies their necessities, facilitates their pleasures, manages their principal concerns, directs their industry, regulates the descent of property, and subdivides their inheritances: what remains, but to spare them all the care of thinking and all the trouble of living?"*[11]

Tocqueville starkly warns of the critical danger in democratic societies: the tendency for individuals to surrender their personal autonomy in exchange for the perceived comfort and security a paternalistic government or individual leader provides. While not overtly tyrannical, this form of governance undermines the citizens' independence and critical thinking abilities, effectively reducing their capacity for self-governance.

What has been discussed previously directly connects to the appeal of strongman leaders like Trump, who offer simplicity amongst complex challenges. The focus groups revealed a longing for a leader who can take control and provide direction, often at the cost of values and democratic norms. The admiration for Trump as a strong, paternal figure who can protect and provide for the nation mirrors Tocqueville's warning. In this light, the tendency to embrace a central authority that promises to manage all aspects of life, ensuring security and prosperity, can be seen as a modern manifestation of the tyranny Tocqueville and Arendt feared.

MAKING THE COUNTRY GREAT AGAIN

The focus group discussions uncover the concerns and fears that historically drive people toward autocrats. These groups express anxiety about the nation's power, with fears about economic decline, loss of cultural identity, and erosion of conservative values.[12] For these individuals, Trump's promise to "Make America Great Again" offers hope and a feeling of nostalgia where a simpler time and a more stable, predictable world existed in their minds. In a conversation about the state of the country and how Trump is the answer that America needs, an older woman in a focus group in Pryor, Oklahoma, stated bluntly:

> "*The United States is getting to be worse than a third-world country.*"

Her concern about national decline was striking and undeniable in every focus group. Undoubtedly, people are more likely to support strongmen when they feel deeply unsettled about their country, culture, and livelihood. Trump's powerful message of "Make America Great Again" effectively taps into these anxieties, positioning him as the leader uniquely capable of reversing this perceived decline. This narrative is a hallmark of authoritarian appeal, resonating with those seeking a forceful and decisive leader.

A recurring theme in discussions with Trump supporters during the focus group was the complex interplay between Arendt's concerns of gullibility and cynicism. Many participants demonstrated a striking willingness to accept falsehoods and misinformation, often due to the deep mistrust they harbored toward traditional sources of truth, such as mainstream media or government institutions. This created a feedback loop, where their skepticism of established authorities made them more susceptible to the narratives offered by Trump and other charismatic figures. As their reliance on these alternative narratives grew, so did their allegiance to the leader, solidifying a closed loop in which both gullibility and cynicism worked together to blur the line between fact and fiction. This dynamic not only fortified their loyalty but also made it increasingly difficult for them to discern objective reality. The result was a potent combination of belief and doubt, where cynicism toward mainstream truth paradoxically fueled unwavering faith in the leader's alternative facts.

Individuals often admired Trump's perceived strength, decisiveness, and willingness to "tell it like it is," even when his statements were factually incorrect or inflammatory. This echoes Arendt's observation that totalitarian leaders often succeed, not despite their lies, but because of them; followers are drawn to the leader's certainty and conviction, regardless of the factual basis.[13] A participant from Mesa, Arizona, stated with conviction:

> *"I just don't know that even the other Republicans have the guts to make big, hard decisions."*

Comments like these, often stirred up emotions and proceeded with a robust defense of Trump as the leader desperately needed for the nation. Many participants, consistently praised Trump for his performance and his commitment to "drain the swamp."

In our discussions, there was widespread distrust in the media, the bureaucracy, and the judicial system, including juries. These trust deficits cannot be ignored and are based on valid concerns. However, such feelings and concerns are often characteristic of authoritarian regimes. In such environments, the leader's narrative becomes the sole source of truth, isolating followers from alternative viewpoints.[14] Another participant from Mesa, Arizona, goes further on this and how Trump has been under constant assault and said:

> *"There is not a candidate, maybe in history that has the guts that he has to pressure....That guy lives under attack every minute of the day, from the far left to the press, to everybody in his own party."*

Authoritarian leaders cultivate a sense of victimhood. By positioning themselves as targets of a biased system, they foster a sense of loyalty among their followers, who see attacks on the leader as attacks on themselves.[15] A particularly telling quote came from a woman in Utah, who advocated on behalf of Trump and how the strongman persona is a good quality by stating:

> *"I like the fact that he's a bully. I mean, I think we need a bully in there."*

Trump's aggressive tactics are admired, which reveals a willingness to accept, or even support, strongman behavior as long as it is directed at perceived enemies or those who are against him. This attitude is consistent with the behavior of followers in totalitarian regimes, where the ends justify the means.[16] A participant in Utah County, Utah, expressed tolerance with Trump's lying and rule-breaking by using a technique of moral rationalization:

> "I think [Trump] was a great leader ... I think all politicians act and lie to get ahead."

A statement like this one shows a willingness to accept moral compromises from Trump as part of a broader cynicism toward elected officials. It connects strongly with Arendt's idea that totalitarian leaders rise by normalizing deception and cultivating an environment where lying is seen as a necessary part of leadership. This undermines trust in democratic norms, creating space for authoritarian practices and strong, decisive leadership that prioritizes action over process and results over principles.[17]

In Pryor, Oklahoma, a participant firmly stated that there exists a prevailing perception that a man is considered the ideal leader, while regrettably, a woman is not perceived as strong as a man. This comparison was made when discussing Trump in relation to other Republican candidates and explaining why they see Trump as a stronger leader. The participant stated:

> "Nikki Haley ... she's a woman ... But the simple fact of it is, the people overseas and those foreign countries will not listen to a woman. They dominate women there.

So why? What makes you think they're going to listen to her when they dominate their own women?"

A statement like this one was not an outlier but rather a commonplace attitude in many of the conversations. It reflects a deeper, possibly unconscious, alignment with an authoritarian mindset. Perspectives like this reinforce patriarchal values and align either knowingly or unknowingly with a desire for a dominant, traditionally male figure to exert control and ensure security both domestically and internationally.

UNDERMINING DEMOCRACY

Our focus group discussions regarding Trump and the strongman mentality expose a troubling erosion of respect for democratic norms. These quotes vividly illustrate how theories of authoritarianism, strongmen, and totalitarianism manifest in today's political landscape. Admiration for Trump's strength, coupled with distrust of institutions, mirrors historical conditions that allowed authoritarian leaders to grow in power.[18] The idea of trusting Trump over the media, courts, or politicians points to a rejection of democratic checks and balances, essential for consolidating power by undermining opposition and oversight. This erosion of trust in institutions creates a vacuum where the leader's word becomes the gospel truth and holds dangerous sway, a critical step toward authoritarian or totalitarian control.[19]

As discussed earlier in the chapter on victimhood and further explored here, Trump's portrayal as a victim, claiming unparalleled mistreatment, solidifies a deep sense of loyalty among his supporters. By positioning himself as an outsider unfairly treated by a corrupt system, he taps into a dynamic environment that was exploited similarly by tyrannical figures in history. This shared sense of persecution fosters collective victimhood among followers, making it increasingly difficult for them to critically evaluate or challenge his actions.[20] The approval of Trump as a "bully" and disregard for rules is especially troubling, signaling acceptance of authoritarian tactics when they serve supporters' goals. This undermines democracy's foundations, which depend on the rule of law and respect for institutional processes. When unethical behavior is tolerated for results, it opens the door to more significant abuses of power.[21] These quotes show that the appeal of authoritarian leadership is deeply tied to identity and emotion, not merely policy preferences. Trump's style fosters a sense of security and belonging, discouraging critical thinking and alternative perspectives, thus reinforcing authoritarian tendencies.

Conversations from our focus groups remind us that authoritarianism's appeal has deep historical roots. Fears and desires driving people toward such leaders persist today, creating fertile ground for eroding democratic norms. Strongmen offer a sense of relief and power but come with grave risks. As people commit to leaders promising order and greatness, they become less willing to question their actions. In democracy, it is vital to preserve institutions that protect freedoms and prevent the concentration of power. Autocratic dangers are not just historical—they are present, and they absolutely can happen here.

CHAPTER 8

Evaluating Fact and Fiction

On October 2th, 2019, in the White House Oval Office, President Trump took credit for one of his most defining labels against the media, though he had used it several times before. Trump said, "I call the fake news now corrupt news because fake news isn't tough enough ... And I'm the one that came up with the term. I'm very proud of it." That phrase quickly became a trademark of Trump's rhetoric and a central talking point of his campaign. While it was initially used to discredit traditional media, its impact reached far beyond a political slogan. For many Americans, "fake news" became a way to dismiss anything that didn't align with their beliefs, creating confusion about what was real and what was not.[1]

In this era, it is easy to feel informed. People watch cable news, scroll through social media, and listen to talk radio, believing they are getting the facts. However, much of what they consume isn't news at all—it is opinion cloaked in the language of truth. Take Sean Hannity with Fox News, for example. Hannity often begins by promising to "follow the facts" but then launches into a bombastic monologue that stirs emotions and reinforces biases without presenting real news.[2] And this is not unique to one side of the political spectrum. Opinionated, highly partisan media outlets have risen across the board, blending opinion with fact. This creates a dangerous environment where people feel informed yet are often misled by voices offering commentary rather than truth.

This chapter explores how the blurring of fact and opinion has made it harder than ever to discern what is real. As misinformation and disinformation spread and trust in institutions declines, political leaders—especially autocrats—capitalize on this confusion to deepen their influence. The result is a crisis where truth becomes elusive, leaving people to navigate a media landscape filled with opinions masquerading as facts.

Ironically, this distortion of reality is the true "fake news"—not the term used to dismiss unfavorable reporting, but the misinformation that weakens our capacity for fruitful public discourse. Today's media landscape has become a battleground of competing narratives, personal beliefs, and ideological allegiances. With an overwhelming amount of information readily available and the rapid dissemination of content through social media, objective facts often struggle to stand firm. This is the real danger: a world where fake news is not just a label but a pervasive force undermining our ability to distinguish fact from fiction.

MISINFORMATION, DISINFORMATION, AND FAKE NEWS

Information is more abundant and accessible than ever before. With a simple click of a button or a swipe on a phone, we can access vast amounts of content with lightning speed. However, the real challenge is no longer finding information but determining whether that information is reliable and valid. This issue has become increasingly complex as the media landscape evolves, blurring the line between truth and falsehood.

Throughout this book, we have explored the reasons for the blurring of truth—from cognitive biases to moral rationalization and other contributing factors. Now, we turn to a more practical question: How does the average person, regardless of political affiliation, navigate this increasingly complex media landscape? In fact, how do all of us—whether supporters of a particular figure or not—make sense of this informational labyrinth? Whether someone's perspective is entirely accurate or not, it is crucial to understand how they perceive the media environment, how they reconcile conflicting information, and how their personal beliefs and allegiances influence their understanding of truth. Significant concepts and terms have emerged in response to these challenges, which are fundamentally important to recognize. Although terms like misinformation, disinformation, and "fake news" are often used interchangeably, each represents a unique aspect of the problem, both in the present day and historically.[3] It's important to understand these terms in order to navigate today's information landscape and make informed judgments.

Misinformation refers to false information shared without malicious intent. It might stem from an error, a misunderstanding, or even a genuine belief that the information is accurate.[4] Often, misinformation spreads because people trust the sources they receive it from—whether a family member, friend, or favorite online channel—without verifying the facts.

In contrast, disinformation involves the intentional spread of false information designed to mislead or manipulate its audience.[5] Disinformation is a tool used by those seeking to create confusion, sow division, and control narratives for political or financial gain. Falsehoods simply erode democratic foundations.[6]

The term "fake news" has also emerged to describe fabricated stories or misleading narratives presented as legitimate journalism. Though originally used to address online falsehoods and conspiracy theories, fake news is now often weaponized in public discourse to discredit unfavorable media, regardless of the accuracy of the content.[7] This shift has led to widespread cynicism and gullibility.[8] It is increasingly challenging for people to trust even the most reputable and reliable news sources, allowing misinformation to hinder critical thinking and impair our ability to assess facts.

One of the challenges goes beyond just identifying fake news but involves recognizing that much of what people consume today is not actual news at all. It's opinion, politically spun analysis, or near-fictional commentary presented in a way that feels factual. This blending of fact and opinion leads people to believe they are informed when, in fact, they are receiving a biased interpretation of events. Here's an example from our focus groups in Mesa, Arizona, where there is a clear disdain toward the media and a severe lack of trust in the press:

> *"It's hard to trust people when you have ... most of the world and the press made up the whole thing about Trump and Russia."*

It is a comment we see often and is deeply emblematic of a larger societal issue: a growing distrust of traditional media and institutions, creating an environment ripe for misinformation. Many participants expressed an outright rejection of mainstream media, as evidenced by one example from a Pryor, Oklahoma, participant:

> *"PBS, MSNBC, New York Times, Forbes, BBC, Washington Post. All these folks reported nonstop against Donald Trump regarding the Russia collusion, which was a bunch of baloney. ... That was part of false accusations that went on, I mean, for years."*

Although beyond the mere consumption of false information, individuals find themselves progressively trapped by their own loyalties—loyalties that blind them to contradictions and weaken their ability to question or reevaluate their views.

THE MODERN PROPAGANDA PLAYBOOK AND ALLEGIANCE

Joseph Goebbels, the Minister of Propaganda in Nazi Germany, famously said, "If you tell a lie big enough and keep repeating it, people will eventually come to believe it."[9] This strategy of manipulation was as much about forging allegiance to Hitler as it was about spreading disinformation and stirring emotion in keeping support strong for the Nazi causes. With this propaganda and disinformation, allegiance became stronger and allowed people to become more receptive to false narratives, justifying even the most heinous actions.

While propaganda has evolved in the modern era, the principles remain the same. Today's misinformation and disinformation campaigns, amplified by social media, operate on similar psychological mechanisms—first by capturing attention, then by fostering emotional connections, and finally by creating a sense of loyalty to an ideology or figure. Once allegiance is cemented, individuals become less likely to engage in critical thinking and more likely to defend their chosen narratives, even in the face of contradictory evidence. Trump capitalized on people's emotional vulnerabilities—particularly their fears, anxieties, and distrust of institutions.

One of Trump's most effective strategies has been his ability to tap into these emotions and frame himself as the only solution to perceived threats. His rhetoric frequently focuses on "enemies" of the people—whether immigrants, the media, or political opponents—stoking fear that without him, America would be overrun by crime, corruption, and chaos. The repetition of these falsehoods intensifies this loyalty. For Trump supporters, the more they hear these claims—whether about election fraud, media bias, or threats to their freedom—the more these ideas become ingrained as truth. This is not simply a matter of believing individual lies but rather adopting a worldview where anything that contradicts Trump's narrative is dismissed as part of a larger conspiracy.[10] His supporters, feeling emotionally invested, often see attacks on Trump as personal attacks on their values and beliefs. This dynamic makes it increasingly difficult for them to engage with facts or alternative viewpoints, as doing so would require them to question not just Trump but their own deeply held convictions. By the way, we all do the same, and perhaps not to the greatest degree or severity, but it is vital to recognize when we dismiss facts, even if they might not align with what we think or believe.

FUELING THE FLAMES OF MISINFORMATION

Misinformation spreads more rapidly today than at any point in history, largely due to the influence of social media and the 24-hour news cycle. Platforms that prioritize engagement, such as Facebook, X (formerly Twitter), and YouTube, have unintentionally become amplifiers of false information.[11] The days when traditional news outlets acted as gatekeepers of verified information are largely behind us. Instead, social media platforms, blogs, and opinion channels flood our screens with competing narratives, making it increasingly difficult to distinguish between what's accurate and what's distorted.

These platforms are designed to keep users engaged, often by promoting content that elicits strong emotional responses, whether the content is accurate or not. As misinformation circulates, it often paves the way for more dangerous narratives, including conspiracy theories and hoaxes. Conspiracy theories, which suggest hidden plots behind major events, thrive in environments where people are unsure whom to trust.[12] During times of political or social upheaval, misinformation can lead to widespread belief in unproven claims, such as election fraud or secret government plots.[13] These theories are appealing because they offer simple explanations for complex situations, playing into the cognitive biases that make individuals more likely to believe information that aligns with their existing beliefs.

What makes misinformation particularly troubling in this context is how it creates a feedback loop. This emotional investment in false narratives creates a continuous cycle where people surround themselves with content that reinforces their beliefs. Social media exacerbates this by showing users more of what they engage with, narrowing their worldview further.[14] A main challenge in the digital era is how people internalize and react to information. Cognitive biases—mental shortcuts that help individuals process complex information quickly—are particularly influential in this landscape.[15] One of the most prominent biases is confirmation bias, where individuals seek out information that aligns with their pre-existing beliefs and dismiss anything that contradicts them.[16] For example, those convinced of widespread voter fraud in the 2020 U.S. election are more likely to consume and share articles, videos, or social media posts that support these claims, regardless of their accuracy. Additionally, motivated reasoning drives individuals to interpret information in a way that reinforces their emotions and ideological leanings.[17] When faced with facts challenging their beliefs, individuals often double down on their original views rather than reconsider them.

For example, as one Mesa, Arizona participant, in a conversation about the election being stolen, particularly in Arizona, stated:

> *"But I know firsthand people in the Arizona election were lying, so I don't trust any of that."*

This phenomenon is known in political behavior studies as the backfire effect, where increased corrections of misinformation harden support for the targeted ideological group.[18] In our focus groups, we pushed people to look at facts, some of which they had not seen before. This is an example of disengaging from facts and locking into original views. Instead of acknowledging the truth when presented with it, people tend to reject or dismiss factual evidence, perceiving it as a threat to their identity or worldview and then locking down or blaming others.[19]

In a similar discussion about the integrity of the election and seeing facts about court cases, voter fraud, and bipartisan attempts at examining the votes for the presidential election, a focus group participant from Pryor, Oklahoma, noted:

> *"And these very people who spoke contrary to him said that there was no election fraud that would overturn the election. They didn't say there wasn't any election fraud. Yeah. And he said*

there was election fraud there. There was election fraud. He didn't lie in effect."

The participant's comment reflects a strong cognitive bias, particularly motivated reasoning, where information is processed to align with their loyalty to Trump. The individual acknowledges that others have stated that no fraud occurred that would overturn the election, yet they interpret this in a way that supports Trump's claim of election fraud. Instead of reconciling the contradictory evidence (that there was no widespread fraud), the participant reframes the narrative. They acknowledge that fraud was found but emphasize that Trump "didn't lie," thus protecting their trust in him.

This psychological element shows how allegiance influences not just beliefs but also the interpretation of facts. Even when confronted with evidence that doesn't align with their worldview, people like this participant reinterpret it to maintain internal consistency and avoid the discomfort of cognitive dissonance. In essence, it is not about discovering the objective truth but about preserving the emotional and ideological investment in a particular figure or narrative.

ALLEGIANCE CAN BE BROKEN

Today, the battle is not just over facts but over belief. The misinformation and disinformation period of our time has shifted the ground beneath us, making allegiance to narratives more powerful than allegiance to truth. The emotional pull that makes us cling to comfortable falsehoods is reasonable to empathize with, given widespread distrust and repeated lies across media sources and leaders who have preyed upon our own weaknesses. However, that does not mean that people can push back and reevaluate.

Allegiance can be broken. Escaping this trap requires more than just learning to recognize falsehoods. It demands that we confront the unsettling reality of our own biases and our willingness to accept convenient truths over uncomfortable facts. In the end, progress stems from fostering a culture where doubt, skepticism, and curiosity are welcomed while being separated from echo chambers and conspiracy theories, which are breeding grounds for manipulation. The next chapter will explore practical steps for regaining clarity in this age of misinformation and distrust. These steps will not only help us avoid the dangerous trap of blind allegiance but also guide us on how to regain our consciousness and critical thinking abilities, which are inherent to us as human beings.

CHAPTER 9

Avoiding and Overcoming
The Totality of Allegiance

We are unquestionably at a critical moment in history. The challenges facing today's democracies are significant and reflect authoritarian tendencies observed in the past and present. These political and ideological challenges strike at the heart of how citizens gather, evaluate, and act on information. In times of political uncertainty, the process of evaluating information becomes not just an intellectual exercise but a moral imperative. The choices we make—whether in voting for a candidate, supporting a specific policy, or aligning ourselves with a movement—depend on how effectively we navigate this landscape of competing facts, perspectives, and emotions.

Understanding the impact of cognitive and social behaviors on the information we analyze is a crucial aspect of the decision-making process. It is imperative to recognize how these behaviors shape our perceptions and responses, especially when engaging with Trump supporters in focus groups. The concepts and theories discussed in this book, along with detailed explanations of how they are put into practice, draw attention to important issues. We also aim to revive critical thinking from the political rhetoric and unquestioning loyalty that we observed over the last year.

The world is witnessing a concerning rise of autocratic regimes, and at the present moment, the United States is teetering on the edge of a precipice. Throughout history and today, authoritarian regimes and totalitarian leaders have relied on controlling information and stifling independent thinking. This often leads to a surge in anti-intellectualism.[1] It is important to recognize that these dynamics can occur in any society.

As citizens, we can resist political and societal pressures by actively controlling how we gather information and critically reflect before reaching conclusions. In the midst of a presidential election in America, it is essential for voters to thoroughly evaluate the policies and leaders at hand. It is equally important to focus on the tools and skills that will enable us to make thoughtful decisions. Regardless of the political context, be it authoritarian or democratic, the process remains constant: We need to gather the most reliable information, critically evaluate it, and allow ourselves the necessary time to reflect, even if it means sitting with discomfort, before reaching decisions. This embodies the very essence of engaged citizenship.

FROM INFORMATION TO DECISION: PRACTICAL TOOLS FOR EVALUATION

When making political decisions, it's important to look beyond reacting to headlines or being swayed by political speeches. To make informed choices about who or what to support, we need to approach information practically and reflectively. This includes using systematic tools that have been developed, which we used as we gathered and later presented the information and facts in our focus groups. These include tools such as the CRAAP and TRAAP models, which help us assess information based on its currency, relevance, authority, accuracy, and purpose.[2]

For example, the CRAAP Test helps assess five critical aspects of information:

Currency: Is the information up to date? This is particularly important when dealing with fast-moving topics such as scientific research or political developments. Outdated information can often lead to poor decisions if the data no longer reflects current realities.

Relevance: Does the information meet your needs? Ask yourself if the content addresses the questions you're trying to answer or provides relevant context to the issue you're considering. This prevents being sidetracked by interesting but unrelated facts.

Authority: Who is the author or source of the information? Are they credible and well-regarded in their field? This helps ensure you are getting information from experts or reputable organizations, not from people or outlets with questionable backgrounds.

Accuracy: Is the information supported by evidence? Is it consistent with other credible sources? Here, cross-checking facts with multiple sources helps verify whether the claims hold up.

Purpose: What is the intention behind the information? Is it trying to inform, persuade, or sell something? Knowing the purpose can help you evaluate any potential bias or motive.

The TRAAP model, an updated version of CRAAP, emphasizes timeliness and adds nuance to evaluating the accuracy and authority of sources.[3] The TRAAP framework extends the critical thinking process by asking readers to closely examine how time-sensitive the information is and whether the authority of the source fits the specific issue at hand. For instance, a health professional would have the authority to discuss medical conditions, but their opinion on a political policy may not carry the same weight.

To further reduce the risk of falling into misinformation traps, the AllSides Media Bias Chart offers a practical tool to gauge the political leanings of various news outlets.[4] Triangulating information—checking multiple sources across the ideological spectrum—helps to ensure that our understanding is balanced and not unduly influenced by biased perspectives. This media literacy is essential in an age where polarized news environments can easily reinforce pre-existing biases.

EVALUATING WITH INTELLECTUAL HUMILITY

The work does not stop at gathering and verifying facts. Information, even when credible, must be engaged with thoughtfully and reflectively. As we take in new perspectives, intellectual humility plays a significant role. It is the recognition that our initial reactions may not always be correct and that our understanding is always evolving. Sitting with new information—especially when it challenges deeply held beliefs—requires patience and the courage to reflect before reacting.[5] In our own research, we encountered moments when participants were given factual information that directly contradicted their support for a leader or a policy.

Some immediately responded in a tribal way to defend Trump, using whataboutisms to bring up the other side for debate. Others were quieter, reserved, and attentively listening, which is the first important step toward recognizing facts.

These different experiences underscore the importance of listening first to understand. True engagement with information requires more than consuming data; it demands the time and intellectual humility to critically analyze and evaluate whether or not the information aligns with reality.[6] This patient reflection—sitting with facts rather than reacting immediately—allows us to avoid the pitfalls of cognitive dissonance and confirmation bias, often leading individuals to reject evidence that challenges their beliefs.[7]

THE ROLE OF AUTHORITY IN EVALUATING FACTS

Another critical aspect of information gathering is the credibility of trusted voices. As we saw in our focus groups, some participants were moved by personal testimonies from individuals who had worked closely with Trump, especially the list of former Cabinet officials who no longer support him.[8]

Statements like those from John Kelly, who described Trump's dishonesty and flawed character, led some to pause and reconsider their support. Supporters sometimes agreed with Trump's character flaws, but in terms of policies and actions as president, those were far and away more important.[9]

However, this openness was not universal. For many, loyalty to Trump as the ultimate authority overshadowed the voices of other leaders and experts. Authority figures, both inside and outside the Republican Party, who spoke out against Trump—whether on policies or principles—were frequently labeled as traitors or RINOs (Republicans in Name Only). Instead of being recognized as credible or principled voices, they were often cast as enemies of Trump.

This reaction highlights the danger of unquestioned authority. In our focus groups, it became clear that for many participants, Trump is seen as the singular source of truth. Regardless of their credentials or experience, anyone who disagrees with him is viewed as untrustworthy.

Critical thinking is eroded as supporters question experts, constitutional processes, and even long-standing principles of governance before they would question Trump. This tendency to place unwavering trust in one individual—at the expense of other trusted voices and institutions—raises serious concerns about the health of democratic discourse.

Focusing on one authority figure to the exclusion of all others signals a more serious problem: the diminishing ability to evaluate information critically. When loyalty to a leader eclipses reason, it becomes increasingly difficult to engage in the thoughtful reflection that democracy requires. It's a reminder of how easily critical thinking can be undermined when authority is concentrated in one person, and the voices of those who challenge that authority are dismissed outright.

HISTORICAL LESSONS ON AUTHORITY AND POLITICAL ALLEGIANCE

As we reflect on this moment, it's important to remember that good, decent people with legitimate concerns can sometimes be drawn to strong leaders who promise solutions. Richard Hamilton's study in *Who Voted for Hitler* reveals how many who supported Hitler were motivated by real fears—economic instability, political disenfranchisement, and a desire for strong leadership.[10]

His work reminds us that people are not driven by ignorance or malice but often by genuine worries about the future. The participants in our focus groups echoed similar concerns—about living expenses, national security, immigration, and their trust in government. These concerns are valid, but history also shows us the importance of critical thinking, especially when leaders offer easy answers.

The danger lies in placing unquestioned trust in any one authority figure. When allegiance becomes absolute, critical thinking erodes. This is not a condemnation of those who follow such leaders but a reminder to stay vigilant and ensure that loyalty does not overshadow reason or disregard moral consequences.

REFLECTION AND ACTION

The culmination of this process is not just understanding information but making informed decisions about where we stand on issues and candidates. In authoritarian environments, citizens are often pressured to act quickly, aligning themselves with those in power. In contrast, a healthy democracy demands that we take the time to reflect and carefully weigh our options. This requires us to sit with facts, to triangulate information through multiple sources, and to critically assess both the data and our own emotional responses.

One of the most important insights from David McRaney is the recognition that changing minds is not a fast process. In his book *How Minds Change*, he emphasizes that real persuasion happens when individuals are given the space to reflect on new information without feeling attacked or pressured to respond immediately.[11] This reinforces the importance of creating environments where we can thoughtfully engage with challenging information rather than react defensively. The key to countering deeply held beliefs, McRaney explains, lies in giving people the opportunity to process information over time, enabling them to reconsider their positions based on thoughtful evaluation rather than emotional loyalty.

In doing so, we empower ourselves to make thoughtful, deliberate decisions rather than reactionary ones. Whether we ultimately support or reject a policy, a leader, or a candidate, the process of reflection ensures that our decisions are grounded in reality rather than swayed by allegiance or emotional manipulation.[12]

In this historic moment, we face the choice between reactionary allegiance or reflective duty as human beings and as citizens. As we navigate these challenges, it is crucial to remember that democracy thrives on informed and thoughtful engagement. The decisions we make now will shape the future of our society. There are some moral and ethical choices ahead for yourself, your neighbors, and collectively as a society. By committing to careful evaluation and reflection of the world around us, we resist the pull of authoritarian pressures and reaffirm our commitment to the democratic principles that guide us. As citizens, we hold the power to either follow this total allegiance or engage with information, people, and reality thoughtfully and critically—ensuring that our choices are grounded in truth, integrity, and respect for our blessed democratic values.

Conclusion

It is essential to return to the central element of our research and work that we have tried our best to articulate to you in this book. The *totality of allegiance* is not just about political loyalty—it is about the erosion of critical thinking, the weakening of democratic norms, and the blurring of moral boundaries. This particular form of allegiance, exemplified by unwavering support for figures like Donald Trump, creates an environment where facts become unsuitable and where personal and civic responsibility can easily be swept aside. Our foremost priority was to handle this research with care and sensitivity, respecting the trust placed in us by the people we encountered. It was important for us to fairly honor the quotes, stories, and struggles of the unique individuals we met with in homes, community centers, and offices across the United States, without critiquing or dishonoring them.

This book has explored in depth how political allegiance can distort perceptions of reality, but it is important to remember that these are real people navigating real economic, social, and moral challenges. The individuals we met and interviewed in our focus groups are not abstract figures defined solely by their political choices. Each of those we met carries within them a wealth of life, passion, and care. These individuals—whom we encountered—are deeply concerned about their families, their jobs, and their communities. It was imperative that we not reduce them to simple supporters of a political figure, and we advocate the same to each of you while still recognizing some of the very theories, concepts, and historical connections discussed throughout these pages. They are human beings motivated by a complex web of concerns, values, and fears. And while their allegiance to Trump may be troubling, we must first recognize the legitimacy of the economic and social policies they care about, the fears that drive them, and the hearts behind their decisions.

TOTALITY OF ALLEGIANCE: HOW LOYALTY ERODES CRITICAL THINKING

Throughout this book, we have explored key theoretical frameworks to explain how deep allegiance to a political figure can cloud judgment and distort moral reasoning. One of the most pressing theories we discussed, which is compounded throughout the other social science theories we leaned on, is cognitive dissonance—the tension that arises when people are faced with information that contradicts their beliefs.[1] We saw this firsthand in our focus groups. Some participants who had been presented with facts that conflicted with their support for Trump were visibly struggling with the implications, but others were able to dismiss the facts and find alternative explanations to support their stance. Most individuals immediately rationalized their positions, seeking to maintain harmony in their beliefs, while others appeared inquisitive and willing to research the facts and points shown and ponder on what they heard and saw during the presentation and conversations.

However, one particular focus group in Utah County, Utah, stands out. A college-aged young man who was considerably reserved compared to his fellow participants finally spoke out after hearing detailed accounts of Trump's moral failings and remarked with some hesitation:

> "I think I need to look into this more. I didn't know this before, and it's unsettling."

His response was not defiant; it was reflective. It was as though something within him had shifted—his once-hardened allegiance had been tested by the weight of new facts. In moments of cognitive dissonance, profound truths emerge to challenge our most deeply held beliefs. These pivotal instances spark critical thinking even in the most unexpected circumstances, compelling us to reevaluate our loyalties in light of undeniable facts.

This young man's response captured a significant moment—a struggle between loyalty and emerging information that he could not easily reconcile. His face showed it. His body language showed it. This allegiance was tested by the weight of these new facts.[2] His demeanor throughout the session was striking, and we made a note of it; it was characterized by discomfort and introspection, which highlighted how confronting uncomfortable truths can spur self-reflection, even when those truths challenge deeply held beliefs. Political loyalties, particularly those intertwined with one's identity, can be difficult to untangle, but moments like this show that change is possible, even in unlikely circumstances.

The dynamics of group loyalty and emotion were also evident. As we discussed the moral implications of supporting Trump, individuals' consistent reactions were a reminder of how political allegiance is often deeply intertwined with moral foundations. Rather than purely logical conclusions, these allegiances are forged through emotional and social bonds, which explains why facts alone are often insufficient to change minds. Jonathan Haidt's work offers insight here, explaining that political allegiances are deeply intertwined with moral foundations, making it difficult for people to accept information that threatens their personal and group identity.[3] Reason often follows emotion, a pattern we frequently saw in our focus groups: participants who felt emotionally connected to their political identity struggled to accept information that conflicted with their support for Trump. This is not unique to Trump supporters, but it underscores the power of moral psychology in shaping political allegiance.

Alongside cognitive dissonance, this book has explored the corrosive effects of tribalism—what has been referred to as the dangerous "us vs. them" dynamic.[4] Tribalism fosters an environment where loyalty to the group supersedes any individual sense of truth or moral responsibility. In our focus groups, this was evident in the way participants clung to their political identities, even when confronted with inconvenient facts. Yet, cracks in this armor were visible. After a fantastic and respectful back-and-forth discussion, a participant in Pryor, Oklahoma, remarked:

> *"Well, this wasn't as bad as I thought it would be."*

What began as a defensive stance (which we absolutely can understand) gave way to a moment of connection, a small but significant step away from the rigid boundaries of tribalism. Another participant in the same group leaned back at the end and said:

> *"This was a good ol' time. I expected this to be rough, but it wasn't as bad as I thought."*

Many participants shared this relief, which underscores the fact that civil dialogue can still thrive even when it challenges deeply held beliefs.

ALLEGIANCE: A UNIVERSAL PHENOMENON

Acknowledging that this phenomenon of total allegiance is not confined to any single political party, ideology, or country is critical. While this book has focused heavily on Trump supporters, the risks of total allegiance exist across the political spectrum, in different parts of the world, and throughout history. Democrats, Socialists, those on the far left, and political actors from every ideological corner are also susceptible to the kind of unquestioning loyalty that weakens critical thinking. This is not a uniquely American problem, nor is it limited to Trump's base.

History is rife with examples of how total allegiance has led to devastating consequences. The rise of fascism in Italy, the tightened totalitarian grip of Nazi Germany, and the authoritarian regimes of North Korea all illustrate how political allegiance can subvert individual morality and lead entire populations into dangerous territory. Political allegiance, when unchecked, becomes a force that erodes the very fabric of democracy. Allegiance to charismatic leaders has repeatedly led societies to abandon democratic norms in favor of authoritarianism.[5]

We see modern examples as well. In Venezuela, for instance, loyalty to authoritarian figures has led to the collapse of democratic processes. Similarly, far-left movements in European nations have shown that allegiance to ideology can override commitment to pluralism and democracy. This phenomenon crosses borders, parties, and ideologies. Though the current moment in the United States with Donald Trump has severe implications, it is part of a larger global trend. The current crisis of allegiance is unique, but historical examples remind us that no political faction or ideology is immune.[6] Allegiance itself is not inherently dangerous. Patriotism and some forms of nationalistic pride are laudable. However, allegiance without scrutiny, an allegiance that blinds people to truth and moral accountability, is inherently dangerous.

THE EROSION OF DEMOCRATIC NORMS

One of the most troubling consequences of total allegiance is the erosion of democratic norms. History teaches us that when loyalty to a leader or ideology takes precedence over commitment to institutions and shared values, democracy begins to fray at the edges. Hannah Arendt warned of this in her seminal work, and she described and analyzed how totalitarian regimes rise through the erosion of truth and the abandonment of shared reality. Her examples offer a chilling parallel to our contemporary moment. In a political landscape where facts are routinely dismissed and authoritarian figures are granted unchecked loyalty, the foundations of democracy become increasingly fragile.[7]

This erosion was evident in the focus groups we conducted. Participants, though deeply concerned about the state of the nation, often placed their faith in a single figure to address their grievances, even at the expense of democratic institutions. This blind loyalty to a strongman, a pattern well-documented in the history of authoritarian regimes, presents a serious threat to the principles of democracy.

When citizens stop questioning their leaders and begin to prioritize loyalty over truth, democracy is on a perilous path. When people begin to lose trust in a fellow citizen, or even a fellow Republican or Democrat for that matter, or struggle to believe juries and judges as fellow citizens, we will continue along a perilous path where respect for each other and the rule of law diminishes. The decline in civic engagement and social trust paves the way for hyper-partisanship and tribalism to thrive, making it harder for people to engage in the kind of open, thoughtful dialogue that strengthens democracy.

Work across disciplines and studies underscores the importance of rebuilding civic institutions that foster trust and community rather than division.[8]

THE EMOTIONAL TOLL OF EMPATHIC LISTENING

Throughout this research, we encountered profound emotional challenges. Conducting these focus groups, often with individuals whose views sometimes clashed with our own, took a heavy emotional toll. But this kind of empathetic engagement was necessary, and that is what we are trained to do: check our biases at the door. We entered each focus group with one goal: to listen—to truly hear what participants had to say. In doing so, we suspended judgment and approached each person with humility, compassion, and absolute openness. This empathy-driven approach enabled us to see the humanity behind their political choices.

Alan Alda's approach to science communication, as outlined in his book *If I Understood You, Would I Have This Look on My Face?*, was instrumental in shaping our method.[9] Alda emphasizes the importance of listening with empathy and understanding before attempting to communicate complex ideas. His belief that genuine connection comes from first hearing the other person shaped our approach to these focus groups. Rather than imposing our views or engaging in debate, we allowed participants to share their stories, defend their beliefs, and express their concerns. This approach, though emotionally taxing, was crucial to the integrity of our research. It reminded us, time and again, that beneath political loyalties are human beings with deeply personal reasons for their choices.

One focus group in Washington, Utah, left a particularly lasting impression. Our host was a man who participated, and he also graciously opened his home to us. The gentleman, serving a mission for the Church of Jesus Christ of Latter-day Saints, requested that we begin the focus session with a heartfelt and moving prayer, setting the tone for a morning of thoughtful discussion. It was strongly evident that there was a shared sense of citizenship, a recognition that we were all bound by our love for our country and our commitment to understanding one another. This moment, simple as it was, underscored the importance of empathy in bridging political divides. It reminded us that, despite our differences, there are values—such as love for country, community, and family—that we all share. Though often overshadowed by political allegiance, these shared values remain the key to fostering understanding and rebuilding democratic trust.

RECOGNIZING HUMANITY AMIDST DIVISION

A takeaway from these focus groups is this: the people we spoke with are not caricatures of political loyalty. They are complex individuals, each with their own struggles, values, and hopes for the future. Many of them voiced legitimate concerns about the economy, cost of living, immigration, abortion, healthcare, and the direction of the country. These are real issues, and dismissing them outright because of the political figures they support does a disservice to the complexity of their humanity.

One participant's words plainly expressed their fears. This shared sentiment was a majority consensus among the group of participants:

> *"I'm not voting for Trump because I think he's perfect, but because I don't see anyone else addressing the issues that matter to me."*

Participants who, despite their allegiance to a controversial figure, felt that their concerns about taxes, job security, and healthcare were not being addressed by anyone else. We noticed that if there were a harmony among the individuals we spoke to, it would be a motto of policies first. In addition, a majority of their statements reflected that a candidate's character matters to some extent, but it's not the prominent factor in their choice for president. Just as importantly, participants possess real fears tied to real lives, and they deserve to be heard—even as we remain critical of how allegiance to a single leader can distort judgment. This tension—between legitimate concerns and the potentially dangerous consequences of unwavering loyalty—defines the complexity of political allegiance.

THE RESPONSIBILITY OF CRITICAL THINKING

As we reflect on these conversations and lessons from history, we now turn to you and ask: What allegiances shape your beliefs? What ideologies or leaders have you aligned yourself with, and do those allegiances hold up under scrutiny? In a moment of great political and social uncertainty, it is not enough to ask these questions of others. We must also ask them of ourselves.

Political allegiance, as we have seen, can be both a force for unity and a trap that blinds us to the truth. Each of us must take the time to question our beliefs, engage with facts, and remain open to the discomfort that comes with challenging long-held loyalties. The preservation of democratic values depends on our collective willingness to think critically, listen empathetically, and maintain a commitment to truth—no matter how inconvenient that truth may be.

There is no doubting the fact that misinformation and disinformation are deepening political divides and reinforcing false beliefs.[10] Rumors and falsehoods, when left unchecked, can harden political allegiances and make it even harder for individuals to accept new information.[11] This phenomenon was evident in our focus groups, where participants often struggled to separate facts from the narratives they had internalized and viewed on highly partisan news media and sources.

By actively engaging with new information and questioning the sources of our beliefs, we can begin to dismantle these false narratives and restore a sense of shared reality.

A PATH FORWARD: EMPATHY, CRITICAL THINKING, AND DEMOCRACY

As we look ahead, the lessons from our research are clear: the *totality of allegiance* poses a profound threat to democratic values, but it is not an insurmountable challenge. We and others before us have cautioned against the dangers of loyalty superseding truth, and prior historical works or current leaders who advocate for this very thing resonate deeply in this moment of history.

But while the risks are grave, there is also hope. The conversations we had, the moments of self-reflection we witnessed, and the empathy we fostered in these focus groups point to a potential way forward. The path forward is rooted in three key principles: empathy, critical thinking, and a renewed commitment to democratic norms.

First, empathy must extend beyond personal and political divides. We must listen to one another—not just to debate but to understand the values, concerns, and fears that shape our views. This kind of empathetic listening is hard and often uncomfortable, but it is the foundation of any meaningful dialogue in a divided society.

Second, critical thinking must be restored as a central pillar of our civic engagement. The erosion of truth and the rise of misinformation have made it easier than ever for allegiance to replace reason. But critical thinking—the willingness to question our own beliefs, to seek out facts, and to engage with new information—is essential to preserving democracy. As we saw in our focus groups, even small moments of doubt or reflection can break through the wall of allegiance. It is these moments of reflection that we must cultivate, both in ourselves and in others.

Finally, a renewed commitment to democracy must guide our actions. Total allegiance to a single leader or ideology risks undermining the very principles upon which democracy is built—pluralism, accountability, and the rule of law. To safeguard these principles, we must be vigilant in defending democratic institutions and norms, even when they are tested by those very political figures we support.

THE SHARED DUTY OF PROTECTING DEMOCRACY

We, as citizens—but also as informed voters—must remember that the responsibility to protect democracy does not lie solely with elected leaders or policymakers. It is a shared duty, one that we must all bear, especially in a blessed republic such as the United States, and only if we can keep it amongst all the challenges, evils, and turmoil that almost insurmountably appear to want our sacred republic gone.

Each of us has the power to engage more deeply in conversations that matter, foster empathy in our interactions, and remain vigilant against the allure of unhesitating allegiance. By doing so, we can resist the erosion of critical thinking and ensure that the values we each stand for continue onward, even when those across the street or in the next state disagree with us. That is the bright spot against the ill-fated route of blind and total allegiance. Disagreement and differences are virtuous when doing so with real intent to understand and accept differences. If we are to preserve democracy in this fraught moment, we must continue to tell these stories, listen with empathy, and engage with the facts, even when they challenge our deepest beliefs.

The responsibility to protect democracy does not rest solely on the shoulders of politicians or institutions. The stories and concerns shared in this book are not mere political anecdotes; they are windows into the struggles of real people navigating complex issues. If we are to preserve democracy, we must engage with these stories, listen empathetically, and foster critical thinking.

As you close this book, we leave you with this thought: democracy's survival depends on our willingness to resist total allegiance. In a world where loyalty to political figures can so easily cloud judgment, our greatest responsibility is to protect the truth, challenge our own beliefs, and engage in the difficult work of defending democratic principles. The future of democracy is not guaranteed—it is something we must actively craft and re-craft each and every day.

It is up to each of us to protect those values and ensure that democracy not only survives but thrives.

Acknowledgments

We are profoundly grateful for the research, collaboration, and writing support from so many wonderful individuals. The hundreds of hours that our talented student research assistants put into this project over the last year, along with developing the survey and focus group procedure, including recruitment and scheduling was immensely helpful. We are proud of these assistants: Enoch Paxton, Kate Huber, Elise Forbes, Rebecca Doucette, Macy Paxton, Sophie Paxton, Anna McConkie, Grace Andros, and Austin Cook. Thank you for sharing your time and efforts during this demanding journey.

The editing and process of getting the book in the form that we can hold in our hands today is due to the enormously helpful insight and work of Alyssa Farnsworth, who is an author's dream editor. Thanks also to Kurt Sandholz for reviewing a few of our chapters and our editorials that were published in preparation for the book launch. To our colleagues at the Marriott School of Business at Brigham Young University and to those in other departments on campus: we are grateful we could bounce ideas off you and gather insight through conversation and fulfilling dialogue to fasten together the scholarly work for this endeavor. We are especially thankful for Erica Miller, who was a phenomenal provider of advice, citations, and blueprints on properly executing the unique research design and process we wanted to accomplish.

We immensely appreciate each of the focus group participants who took time out of their day and sacrificed a couple of hours so we could conduct this research and more clearly understand and explain individuals' support for their candidate of choice for President of the United States. We obviously could not have done this research without you. Thank you.

Last of all, our families are everything to us, and we are blessed beyond measure by their love and support. Thank you for letting us put our shoulder to the wheel to remove this burden we both felt intensely. Tackling this enormously important project put a great emotional strain on both of us. We could not have accomplished this without your grace and reassurance. Thank you, Jessica and Kristi, for your labors of love that may be behind the scenes but critical to this stand for democracy.

Appendix

Focus Group and Survey Questions

QUESTIONS ON FACTS ABOUT STOLEN ELECTION

Q1. How familiar are you with the information that was just shown?
(1- Not at all familiar to 5- Entirely familiar)

Q2. How valid do you think the information is?
(1- Not at all valid to 5- Entirely valid)

Q3. To what extent did this information cause you to question your support for Trump receiving the GOP nomination in 2024?
(1- Not at all valid to 5- A great deal)

Q4. What do you think about the statements and/or the information shared in the video?
(Open- text)

QUESTIONS ON FACTS ABOUT TRUMP'S CHARACTER

Q5. How familiar are you with the information that was just shown?
(1- Not at all familiar to 5- Entirely familiar)

Q6. How valid do you think the information is?
(1- Not at all valid to 5- Entirely valid)

Q7. To what extent did this information cause you to question your support for Trump receiving the GOP nomination in 2024?
(1- Not at all valid to 5- A great deal)

Q8. What do you think about the statements and/or the information shared in the video?
(Open- text)

CIVIC KNOWLEDGE TEST

Q9. Which right is guaranteed by the Second Amendment of the Constitution of the United States?
[] The right to a fair trial.
[] The right to freedom of speech.
[] The right to keep and bear arms.
[] The right to vote for public officials.

Q10. Please list the three branches of the U.S. government. (Please list as many as you can think of.)
(Open-text)

Q11. Which party currently has the most members in the United States House of Representatives?
[] Republicans
[] Democrats
[] Not sure/ Don't know

Q12. What office does John Roberts currently hold? (If you don't know, simply type "Don't know")
(Open-text)

APPENDIX 169

Q13. How long is one term for a U.S. Senator?
[] Two Years
[] Four Years
[] Six Years
[] Ten Years
[] Not sure/Don't know

Q14. If the President and Supreme Court differ on whether an action by the President is constitutional, who has the final responsibility for determining if the action is constitutional- (the president), (Congress), or (the Supreme Court), or are you not sure?
[] President
[] Congress
[] Supreme Court
[] Not sure/Don't know

Q15. In what year was the U.S. Constitution ratified?
[] 1776
[] 1865
[] 1620
[] 1789

Q16. Toward the end of the Revolutionary War, George Washington had to quell a rebellion among his troops against Congress because they hadn't been paid. Where did he give his famous speech in which he admonished them to remember the goals for which they fought?
[] New York City, New York
[] Newburgh, New York
[] Hampton, Virginia
[] Washington, D.C.

PARTICIPANT INFORMATION

Q17. With which political party do you most identify?
[] Democratic Party
[] Republican Party
[] Independent or unaffiliated
[] Other (specify)

Q18. Which of the following categories best describes your political ideology? Ideology
[] Strongly Liberal
[] Liberal
[] Slightly Liberal
[] Middle of the Road
[] Slightly Conservative
[] Conservative
[] Strongly Conservative

Q19. On average, how often do you read the news section of the newspaper, watch news coverage on television, read news content on the Internet, or listen to news-related podcasts?
[] Never
[] Less than once a month
[] Once a month
[] 2-3 times a month
[] Once a week
[] 2-3 times a week
[] Daily

Q20. How often do you use social media (e.g. Facebook, Twitter) to get your news?
[] Never
[] Less than once a week
[] Once a week
[] 2-3 times a week
[] Once a day
[] 2-3 times a day
[] More than 3 times a day

Q21. In the past MONTH, did you receive your political news from any of the following social media platforms: (Check all that apply)
[] Facebook
[] Twitter (X)
[] Truth Social
[] YouTube
[] Reddit
[] Parler
[] Rumble
[] Telegram
[] Instagram
[] Other (specify)

APPENDIX 171

Q22. In the past MONTH, did you receive your political news from any of the following: (Check all that apply)
[] ABC News
[] CBS News
[] NBC News
[] Breitbart
[] Politico
[] CNN
[] Huffington Post
[] Fox News
[] Washington Post
[] Joe Rogan Experience
[] PBS
[] NPR
[] New York Times
[] MSNBC
[] Newsmax
[] One America News (OAN)
[] Vox
[] Other (specify)

Q23. What was the estimated annual income for your household in 2022:
[] Less than $25,000
[] At least $25,000 but less than $50,000
[] At least $50,000 but less than $75,000
[] At least $75,000 but less than $100,000
[] At least $100,000 but less than $125,000
[] At least $125,000 or more

Q24. How important is religion in your life?
[] Not at all important
[] Slightly important
[] Moderately important
[] Very important
[] Extremely important

Q25. What is your current marital status?
[] Married
[] Widowed
[] Divorced
[] Separated
[] Never married

Q26. What type of community do you live in?
[] Rural area
[] Small city or town
[] Suburb near a large city
[] Large city

Q27. What is the highest level of education you have COMPLETED?
[] Less than HS diploma
[] HS diploma/GED
[] Some college (no degree)
[] Associate's degree
[] Bachelor's degree
[] Graduate degree

Q28. Which of the following best describes your race? (Please check one).
[] White
[] Black
[] Hispanic
[] Asian
[] American Indian/Alaskan Native
[] Other Race (specify)

Q29. Which of the following best describes your gender?
[] Male
[] Female
[] Prefer not to self-describe (Specify)
[] Prefer not to answer

PLEASE INDICATE YOUR LEVEL OF AGREEMENT WITH THE FOLLOWING STATEMENTS:

Q30. Political divisiveness is a major problem in the U.S.
(1- Strongly disagree to 5- Strongly agree)

Q31. I have little issue affording my living expenses.
(1- Strongly disagree to 5- Strongly agree)

Q32. Violent actions against the government are sometimes justified.
(1- Strongly disagree to 5- Strongly agree)

Q33. Crime is a significant problem in my community
(1- Strongly disagree to 5- Strongly agree)

Q34. Women have the same rights as men to work and study outside of their home.
(1- Strongly disagree to 5- Strongly agree)

Q35. The U.S. 2020 presidential election outcome was stolen.
(1- Strongly disagree to 5- Strongly agree)

2024 ELECTION QUESTIONS

Q36. What is the probability that you will be supporting Donald Trump for the GOP nomination for president for 2024?
- [] Greater than 90 percent
- [] 75 to 90 percent
- [] 50 to 75 percent
- [] Below 50 percent

Q37. Please rank your first three candidates for the 2024 GOP Primary.

1st Choice_____
2nd Choice_____
3rd Choice_____

Q38. What are your top two reasons for supporting Trump for the GOP nomination for president in 2024?
(Open-text)

Q39. What is your biggest concern in supporting Donald Trump for the GOP nomination for President in 2024?
(Open-text)

Q40. What do the indictments against Donald Trump in Florida involve?
(Open-text)

Notes

Authors' Notes
1. Mark Twain. *The Innocents Abroad*. Penguin, 2007.
2. Immanuel Kant. *What is Enlightenment?* (1784). Translated by Ted Humphrey, Hackett Publishing, 1992.
3. John Adams, *Wemms Trial*, December 1770.
4. Theodore Roosevelt, Citizens in the Republic Speech, at the Sorbonne, Paris, April 23, 1910.

Introduction
1. Kathleen Hall Jamieson, Matthew Levendusky, and Josh Pasek. "'Stop the Steal': The Rhetoric of Electoral Delegitimacy," in *Democracy amid Crises: Polarization, Pandemic, Protests, and Persuasion* (New York: Oxford Academic, 2023).
2. Jason Stanley. *How Fascism Works: The Politics of Us and Them*. Random House, 2018.
3. Arezou Rezvani. "Jan. 6 Rioter Says Trump Should Face the Same Fate as Those Who Stormed the Capitol," *NPR: Morning Edition*, 2023. https://www.npr.org/2023/08/04/1192070242/jan-6-rioter-says-trump-should-face-the-same-fate-as-those-who-stormed-the-capitol.

Chapter 1: The Research Study
1. Snowball sampling is a method often used in qualitative research to recruit participants through referrals from initial subjects, expanding the participant pool through social networks.
2. California State University. "CRAAP Test." Meriam Library, 2010.
3. Australian National University. "TRAAP Model: Updated Version of CRAAP Test." 2018.
4. Norman K. Denzin. Discussion on the power of qualitative research, in *The Sage Handbook of Qualitative Research*, 2011.
5. Udo Kuckartz. *Qualitative Text Analysis: A Guide to Methods, Practice & Using Software.* 2014.
6. VERBI Software. *MAXQDA 2022.* Berlin: VERBI Software, 2021.
7. Leon Festinger. *A Theory of Cognitive Dissonance.* Stanford University Press, 1957.
8. R. S. Nickerson. "Confirmation Bias: A Ubiquitous Phenomenon in Many Guises," *Review of General Psychology*, 1998.
9. C. S. Taber and M. Lodge. "Motivated Skepticism in the Evaluation of Political Beliefs," *American Journal of Political Science*, 2006.
10. Albert Bandura. "Moral Disengagement in the Perpetuation of Inhumanities," *Personality and Social Psychology Review* 3, no. 3 (1999): 193-209.
11. Jason Stanley. *How Fascism Works: The Politics of Us and Them.* Random House, 2018.

Chapter 2: The Trump Phenomenon
1. White House. "Grover Cleveland." www.whitehouse.gov/about-the-white-house/presidents/grover-cleveland/
2. Coeur d'Alene Press. "Trump's Long List of Firsts," *Coeur d'Alene Press*, December 2, 2022.
3. Cas Mudde. *The Far Right Today.* Polity, 2019.
4. Shaun Walker, Tom Phillips, and Jon Henley. "End of Trump Era Deals Heavy Blow to Rightwing Populist Leaders Worldwide," *The Guardian*, November 11, 2020. https://www.theguardian.com/us-news/2020/nov/11/end-trump-era-blow-rightwing-populist-leaders-worldwide-biden-victory-brazil-hungary
5. Corey Robin. *The Reactionary Mind: Conservatism from Edmund Burke to Donald Trump.* Oxford University Press, 2017.
6. Cailin O'Connor and James Owen Weatherall. *The Misinfor-*

mation Age: How False Beliefs Spread. Yale University Press, 2019.
7. Hannah Arendt. *The Origins of Totalitarianism.* Harcourt, Brace & Co., 1951.
8. Robert Yoon. "Trump's Drumbeat of Lies About 2020 Election Keeps Getting Louder. Here are the Facts," *Associated Press*, August 27, 2023. https://apnews.com/article/trump-2020-election-lies-debunked-4fc26546b07962fdbf-9d66e739fbb50d
9. Leon Festinger. *A Theory of Cognitive Dissonance.* Stanford University Press, 1957.
10. Victor D. Hanson. *The Case for Trump.* Basic Books, 2024.
11. Fred C. Trump III. *All in the Family: The Trumps and How We Got This Way.* Gallery Books, 2024.
12. Cassidy Hutchinson. *Enough.* Simon and Schuster, 2023.
13. Maggie Haberman. *Confidence Man: The Making of Donald Trump and the Breaking of America.* Penguin Press, 2022.
14. Steven Hassan. *The Cult of Trump: A Leading Cult Expert Explains How the President Uses Mind Control.* Simon and Schuster, 2019.
15. Tom Schaller and Paul Waldman. *White Rural Rage: The Threat to American Democracy.* Basic Books, 2020.
16. Brian Rees. *How Reasonable Americans Could Support Trump: Helping Liberals Understand the MAGAverse.* Independently Published, 2021.
17. Russell Moore. *Losing Our Religion: An Altar Call for Evangelical America.* Penguin Random House, 2022.
18. John Hibbing. *The Securitarian Personality: What Really Motivates Trump's Base and Why It Matters for the Post-Trump Era.* Oxford University Press, 2020.
19. Dan Merica and Sophie Tatum. Clinton Expresses Regret for Saying 'Half' of Trump Supporters are 'Deplorables,'" *CNN.* September 12, 2016. https://www.cnn.com/2016/09/09/politics/hillary-clinton-donald-trump-basket-of-deplorables/index.html

Chapter 3: Moral Rationalization
1. Jacob Hess. "Many Conservative Republicans Deeply Opposed Trump. Now They Strongly Support Him. What Changed?" *Deseret News*, July 17, 2024. https://www.deseret.com/politics/2024/07/17/many-conservative-republicans-

deeply-opposed-trump-now-they-strongly-support-him-what-changed/
2. Lee Moran. "Lindsey Graham Admits There's 1 Major Problem with Republicans," *Huffington Post*, 2024. https://www.huffpost.com/entry/lindsey-graham-problem-with-republicans_n_66b1ee64e4b0a6fdbe35ef9e
3. Albert Bandura, Claudio Barbaranelli, Gian Vittorio Caprara, and Concetta Pastorelli. "Mechanisms of Moral Disengagement in the Exercise of Moral Agency," *Journal of Personality and Social Psychology* 71, no. 2 (1996): 364.
4. David Matza and Gresham Sykes. "Techniques of Neutra—ization: A Theory of Delinquency," *American Sociological Review* 22, no. 6 (1957): 664–670.
5. Ann E. Tenbrunsel and David M. Messick. "Ethical Fading: The Role of Self-Deception in Unethical Behavior," *Social Justice Research* 17 (2004): 223–236.
6. William Von Hippel and Robert Trivers. "The Evolution and Psychology of Self-Deception," *Behavioral and Brain Sciences* 34, no. 1 (2011): 1–16.
7. Leon Festinger. *A Theory of Cognitive Dissonance*. Stanford University Press, 1957.
8. David Matza and Gresham Sykes. "Techniques of Neutralization: A Theory of Delinquency," *American Sociological Review* 22, no. 6 (1957): 664–670.
9. Albert Bandura. "Moral Disengagement in the Perpetuation of Inhumanities," *Personality and Social Psychology Review* 3, no. 3 (1999): 193–209.
10. Albert Bandura. *Social Foundations of Thought and Action*. Englewood Cliffs, NJ: Prentice-Hall, 1986, pp. 23–28.
11. Bradley Agle, Aaron Miller, and Bill O'Rourke. *The Business Ethics Field Guide*. Provo, UT: Merit Leadership and the Wheatley Institution, 2016, pp. 223–224
12. Denis Ribeaud and Manuel Eisner. "Are Moral Disengagement, Neutralization Techniques, and Self-Serving Cognitive Distortions the Same? Developing a Unified Scale of Moral Neutralization of Aggression," *International Journal of Conflict and Violence* (IJCV) 4, no. 2 (2010): 298–315.
13. Caitlyn Oprysko. "'I Don't Take Responsibility at All': Trump Deflects Blame for Coronavirus Testing Fumble," *Politico*, March 13, 2024. https://www.politico.com/news/2020/03/13/trump-coronavirus-testing-128971
14. Dylan Matthews. "Trump's Refusal to Take Responsibility is

a Deep Moral Failure," *Vox*, 2017. https://www.vox.com/policy-and-politics/2017/10/18/16495288/trump-responsibility
15. Harry S. Truman Library and Museum. "The Buck Stops Here Desk Sign." https://www.trumanlibrary.gov/education/trivia/buck-stops-here-sign
16. Rev. "Trump Addresses National Association of Black Journalists." https://www.rev.com/blog/transcripts/trump-addresses-national-association-of-black-journalists

Chapter 4: Tribalism
1. Donald Trump. Remarks at Campaign Rally, Phoenix, AZ, August 22, 2017.
2. Donald Trump. "Remarks at CPAC," Conservative Political Action Conference, February 29, 2020.
3. Henri Tajfel. *Human Groups and Social Categories*. Cambridge: Cambridge University Press, 1981.
4. Jonathan Haidt. *The Righteous Mind: Why Good People Are Divided by Politics and Religion*. New York: Pantheon, 2012.
5. Eli Pariser. *The Filter Bubble: What the Internet Is Hiding From You*. New York: Penguin Press, 2011.
6. Jason Stanley. *How Fascism Works: The Politics of Us and Them*. New York: Random House, 2018.
7. Adolf Hitler. *Mein Kampf*. Translated by Ralph Manheim. Boston: Houghton Mifflin, 1943.
8. Joseph McCarthy. "Enemies from Within," Speech Delivered in Wheeling, West Virginia, February 9, 1950.
9. Shaun Walker, "George Soros: Orbán Turns to Familiar Scapegoat as Hungary Rows with EU," *The Guardian*, December 5, 2020.
10. Donald Trump. Remarks at Campaign Rally, Phoenix, AZ, August 22, 2017.
11. Paul Farhi, "New Sudy Says Trump Has 'Dangerously Undermined Truth' with Attacks on News Media," *Washington Post*, April 16, 2020. https://www.washingtonpost.com/lifestyle/media/new-study-says-trump-has-dangerously-undermined-truth-with-attacks-on-news-media/2020/04/15/4152f81c-7f2d-11ea-9040-68981f488eed_story.html

Chapter 5: Victimhood
1. Hannah Arendt. *The Origins of Totalitarianism*. Harcourt, 1951.
2. Jason Stanley. *How Fascism Works: The Politics of Us and Them*. Random House, 2018.
3. Roger Eatwell and Matthew Goodwin. *National Populism: The Revolt Against Liberal Democracy*. Penguin UK, 2018.
4. Jason Stanley. *How Fascism Works: The Politics of Us and Them*. Random House, 2018.
5. Daniel Bar-Tal, Liat Chernyak-Hai, Noa Schori, and Atara Gundar. "A Sense of Self-Perceived Collective Victimhood in Intractable Conflicts," *International Review of the Red Cross* 91, no. 874 (2009): 229-258.
6. Ibid.
7. Vamik D. Volkan. *Bloodlines: From Ethnic Pride to Ethnic Terrorism*. Farrar, Straus and Giroux, 1997.
8. Nicole Hemmer. *Messengers of the Right: Conservative Media and the Transformation of American Politics*. University of Pennsylvania Press, 2016.
9. Ian Kershaw. *Hitler: A Biography*. W. W. Norton & Company, 2008.
10. Richard J. Evans. *The Coming of the Third Reich*. Penguin Books, 2004.
11. Edward Lempinen. "Fascism Shattered Europe a Century Ago — and Historians Hear Echoes Today in the U.S." UC Berkeley Research. September 2024. https://vcresearch.berkeley.edu/news/fascism-shattered-europe-century-ago-and-historians-hear-echoes-today-us
12. Ibid.
13. BBC. "Capitol Riots Timeline: What Happened on 6 January 2021," August 1, 2023. https://www.bbc.com/news/world-us-canada-56004916

Chapter 6: Conmen, Cults, and Those Who Follow
1. Karen Halttunen. *Confidence Men and Painted Women: A Study of Middle-Class Culture in America, 1830–1870*. Yale University Press, 1982, pp. 6-7.
2. Herman Melville. *The Confidence Man: His Masquerade*. 1857.
3. Maria Konnikova. *The Confidence Game: Why We Fall for It Every Time*. Viking, 2016.
4. Herman Melville. *The Confidence Man: His Masquerade*.

NOTES 181

1857.
5. Maria Konnikova. *The Confidence Game: Why We Fall for It Every Time.* Viking, 2016.
6. Mitchell Zuckoff. *Ponzi's Scheme: The True Story of a Financial Legend.* Random House, 2006.
7. Diana B. Henriques. *The Wizard of Lies: Bernie Madoff and the Death of Trust.* St. Martin's Press, 2011.
8. Leon Festinger. *A Theory of Cognitive Dissonance.* Stanford University Press, 1957.
9. Max Weber. *The Theory of Social and Economic Organization.* Oxford University Press, 1947.
10. Robert B. Zajonc. "Attitudinal Effects of Mere Exposure," *Journal of Personality and Social Psychology*, 1968.
11. Delroy L. Paulhus and Kevin M. Williams. "The Dark Triad of Personality: Narcissism, Machiavellianism, and Psychopathy," *Journal of Research in Personality*, 2002.
12. Ibid.
13. Steven Hassan. *The Cult of Trump: A Leading Cult Expert Explains How the President Uses Mind Control.* Simon & Schuster, 2019.
14. Alice Herman. "She Was in Trump's Maga Cult – Now She's Fighting Far-Right Extremism," *The Guardian*, June 8, 2024. https://www.theguardian.com/us-news/ng-interactive/2024/jun/08/trump-republican-party-far-right-extremism
15. Ibid.
16. Abbey Marshall. "Trump Botches a Boast About Giving Away His Presidential Salary," *Politico*, October 21, 2019. https://www.politico.com/news/2019/10/21/trump-presidential-salary-053366
17. Bill Gindlesperger. "Trump's Business Acumen: We Need to Call It Like It Is," *Public Opinion*, September 7, 2022. https://www.publicopiniononline.com/story/opinion/columnists/2022/09/07/when-it-comes-to-business-former-president-trump-track-record-dismal/65474745007/
18. Steven Hassan. *The Cult of Trump: A Leading Cult Expert Explains How the President Uses Mind Control.* Simon & Schuster, 2019.
19. Ibid.
20. Robert B. Zajonc. "Attitudinal Effects of Mere Exposure," *Journal of Personality and Social Psychology*, 1968.

Chapter 7: Authoritarianism and the Strongman

1. Ian Kershaw. *Hitler: 1889-1936 Hubris*. W.W. Norton & Company, 1998.
2. Hannah Arendt. *The Origins of Totalitarianism*. Harcourt, Brace & Co., 1951.
3. Ibid.
4. Robert Service. *Stalin: A Biography*. Belknap Press, 2004.
5. Stephen Kotkin. *Stalin: Volume I: Paradoxes of Power, 1878-1928*. Penguin Press, 2014.
6. Steven Levitsky and Daniel Ziblatt. *How Democracies Die*. Crown Publishing, 2018.
7. Takis S. Pappas. *Populism and Liberal Democracy: A Comparative and Theoretical Analysis*. Oxford University Press, 2019.
8. Timothy Snyder. *The Road to Unfreedom: Russia, Europe, America*. Tim Duggan Books, 2018.
9. Ian Kershaw. *Hitler: 1889-1936 Hubris*. W.W. Norton & Company, 1998.
10. Yascha Mounk. T*he People vs. Democracy: Why Our Freedom Is in Danger and How to Save It*. Harvard University Press, 2018.
11. Alexis de Tocqueville. *Democracy in America*. Penguin Books, 2001.
12. Pippa Norris and Ronald Inglehart. *Cultural Backlash: Trump, Brexit, and Authoritarian Populism*. Cambridge University Press, 2019.
13. Hannah Arendt. *The Origins of Totalitarianism*. Harcourt, Brace & Co., 1951.
14. Steven Levitsky and Daniel Ziblatt. *How Democracies Die*. Crown Publishing, 2018.
15. Ruth Ben-Ghiat. *Strongmen: Mussolini to the Present*. W. W. Norton & Company, 2020.
16. Juan J. Linz. *Totalitarian and Authoritarian Regimes*. Lynne Rienner Publishers, 2000.
17. Steven Levitsky and Daniel Ziblatt. *How Democracies Die*. Crown Publishing, 2018.
18. Yascha Mounk. *The People vs. Democracy: Why Our Freedom Is in Danger and How to Save It*. Harvard University Press, 2018.
19. Timothy Snyder. *The Road to Unfreedom: Russia, Europe, America*. Tim Duggan Books, 2018.
20. Ruth Ben-Ghiat. Strongmen: *Mussolini to the Present.* W. W.

Norton & Company, 2020.
21. Juan J. Linz. *Totalitarian and Authoritarian Regimes.* Lynne Rienner Publishers, 2000.

Chapter 8: Evaluating Fact and Fiction
1. Alex Woodward. "'Fake News': A Guide to Trump's Favourite Phrase – and the Dangers It Obscures," *Independent*, October 2, 2020. https://www.independent.co.uk/news/world/americas/us-election/trump-fake-news-counter-history-b732873.html
2. Phil Owen. "Hannity Mocked for Admitting He Doesn't Fact Check Anything He Says on His Show," *Yahoo Entertainment*, November 30, 2020. https://www.yahoo.com/entertainment/hannity-mocked-admitting-doesn-t-044159245.html
3. Alex Woodward. "'Fake News': A Guide to Trump's Favourite Phrase – and the Dangers It Obscures," *Independent*, October 2, 2020. https://www.independent.co.uk/news/world/americas/us-election/trump-fake-news-counter-history-b732873.html
4. Sander van der Linden. *Foolproof: Why Misinformation Infects Our Minds and How to Build Immunity.* Norton & Company, 2023.
5. Barbara McQuade. *How Disinformation is Sabotaging America: Attack from Within.* HarperCollins, 2022.
6. Ibid.
7. Media Matters. "Understanding the Fake News Universe: A Guide to Fake News Terminology," *Media Matters*, December 12, 2016. https://www.mediamatters.org/fake-news/understanding-fake-news-universe
8. Hannah Arendt. *The Origins of Totalitarianism.* Harcourt, Brace & Co., 1951.
9. Joseph Goebbels. "If You Tell a Lie Big Enough and Keep Repeating It…" (Nazi Propaganda, 1939).
10. Dan P. McAdams. "The Mass Psychology of Trumpism," *New Lines Magazine*, February 21, 2024. https://newlinesmag.com/argument/the-mass-psychology-of-trumpism/
11. Soroush Vosoughi, Deb Roy, and Sinan Aral. "The Spread of True and False News Online," *Science*, March 2018.
12. Graham Lawton. "Conspiracy Theories," *New Scientist*. https://www.newscientist.com/definition/conspiracy-theories/
13. Sander van der Linden. *Foolproof: Why Misinformation Infects Our Minds and How to Build Immunity.* Norton & Company, 2023.
14. Matteo Cinelli, Gabriele De Francisci Morales, Alessandro

Galeazzi, Walter Quattrociocchi, and Michele Starnini. "The Echo Chamber Effect on Social Media," *Proceedings of the National Academy of Sciences*, 118, no. 9 (2021): e2023301118.
15. R. S. Nickerson. "Confirmation Bias: A Ubiquitous Phenomenon in Many Guises," *Review of General Psychology*, 1998.
16. Ibid.
17. C. S. Taber and M. Lodge. "Motivated Skepticism in the Evaluation of Political Beliefs," *American Journal of Political Science*, 2006.
18. Brendan Nyhan and Jason Reifler. "When Corrections Fail: The Persistence of Political Misperceptions," *Political Behavior*, 2010.
19. Ibid.

Chapter 9: Avoiding and Overcoming *The Totality of Allegiance*
1. Hannah Arendt. *The Origins of Totalitarianism*. Harcourt, 1951.
2. California State University. "CRAAP Test." Meriam Library, 2010.
3. Australian National University. "TRAAP Model: Updated Version of CRAAP Test." 2018.
4. AllSides. Media Bias Chart. https://www.allsides.com/media-bias/media-bias-chart
5. Julia Galef. *The Scout Mindset: Why Some People See Things Clearly and Others Don't*. Penguin, 2021.
6. Daniel Kahneman. *Thinking, Fast and Slow*. Farrar, Straus and Giroux, 2011.
7. Carol Tavris and Elliot Aronson. *Mistakes Were Made (But Not by Me)*. Houghton Mifflin Harcourt, 2007.
8. Steve Benen. "Half of Trump's Former Cabinet Secretaries Haven't Backed His 2024 Bid," *MSNBC*, August 5, 2024. https://www.msnbc.com/rachel-maddow-show/maddowblog/half-trumps-former-cabinet-secretaries-havent-backed-2024-election-rcna165185
9. Marina Pitofsky. "John Kelly Called Trump the Most Flawed Person He's Ever Met: Report," *The Hill*, November 16, 2020. https://thehill.com/homenews/news/521507-john-kelly-called-trump-the-most-flawed-person-hes-ever-met-report/
10. Richard F. Hamilton. *Who Voted for Hitler?*. Vol. 705. Princeton University Press, 2014.
11. David McRaney. *How Minds Change: The Surprising Science of Belief, Opinion, and Persuasion*. Portfolio, 2022.

12. Sander van der Linden. *Foolproof: Why Misinformation Infects Our Minds and How to Build Immunity.* Norton & Company, 2023.

Conclusion
1. Leon Festinger. *A Theory of Cognitive Dissonance.* Stanford University Press, 1957.
2. Carol Tavris and Elliot Aronson. *Mistakes Were Made (But Not by Me).* Houghton Mifflin Harcourt, 2007.
3. Jonathan Haidt. *The Righteous Mind: Why Good People Are Divided by Politics and Religion.* Vintage, 2012.
4. Jason Stanley. *How Fascism Works: The Politics of Us and Them.* Random House, 2018.
5. Robert Paxton. *The Anatomy of Fascism.* Vintage, 2005.
6. Timothy Snyder. *On Tyranny: Twenty Lessons from the Twentieth Century.* Tim Duggan Books, 2017.
7. Hannah Arendt. *The Origins of Totalitarianism.* Harcourt, 1951.
8. Robert D. Putnam. *Bowling Alone: The Collapse and Revival of American Community.* Simon & Schuster, 2000.
9. Alan Alda. *If I Understood You, Would I Have This Look on My Face?: My Adventures in the Art and Science of Relating and Communicating.* Random House, 2017.
10. Sander van der Linden. *Foolproof: Why Misinformation Infects Our Minds and How to Build Immunity.* Basic Books, 2023.
11. Cass Sunstein. *On Rumors: How Falsehoods Spread, Why We Believe Them, and What Can Be Done.* Farrar, Straus and Giroux, 2009.

Index

Adair, Oklahoma, 12
Adams, John 9, 16
Alabama, 28
Alda, Alan, 157
AllSides Media Bias Chart, 143
anti-intellectualism, 27, 140
Arendt, Hannah 9, 14–15, 114–115, 119–121, 123, 155
Arizona, 26, 29, 36, 43, 49, 52–53, 84, 96, 110, 121–122, 131, 136
authoritarianism, 16, 21, 23, 113, 115–117, 119, 121, 123–125, 155
autocratic regimes, 15, 140
Biden, Joe 21
Bolsonaro, Jair 49, 116
Brigham Young University, 16, 19, 22–23, 166
Buchenwald, 13–14
California, 28
Capitol Riot, 28, 30, 55, 92
charismatic relationship, 20
Church of Jesus Christ of Latter-day Saints, 17, 158
Cleveland, Grover 47

CNN, 12, 171
cognitive bias, 32, 137
cognitive dissonance, 29, 42, 60–61, 103, 106, 108–109, 111, 137, 144, 151–153
confirmation bias, 42–43, 76–77, 82, 84–85, 135, 144
conspiracy theories, 30, 130, 134, 138
critical thinking, 15, 58, 76–77, 85, 99, 101, 111, 119, 125, 131, 133, 138, 140, 142, 145–146, 149–150, 152, 154, 160–163
cult of personality, 116
cultural shifts, 27, 88
Dachau, 17, 23
deep state, 51, 90
dehumanization, 21, 62
democracy, 15–16, 21, 31, 48, 55, 58, 117, 124–126,
democratic erosion, 48
Democratic Party, 169
democratic values, 32, 148, 160–161
denial of responsibility, 63
disinformation campaigns, 133

disinformation, 128–130, 132–133, 137, 160
economic challenges, 27
enlightenment, 11, 13–14
ethical behavior, 20, 29
ethical fading, 60
ethical neutralization, 60–61, 63
Ettersberg Hill, 13
euphemistic labeling, 62
Evangelical Christianity, 56
Facebook, 134, 170
fake news, 51, 66, 74, 80, 127–131
falsehood, 12, 15, 25, 31–32, 70, 115, 120, 129–130, 133, 138, 160
Fascism, 16, 88, 93, 154
focus groups, 22, 26–27, 35–37, 39–45, 52, 66, 80, 82, 119, 125, 131, 136, 140–141, 144–146, 150–151, 153, 156–158, 160–162
Fox News, 12, 51, 92, 128, 171
Goebbels, Joseph, 132
Goethe, Johann Wolfgang 13
Haberman, Maggie, 55
Hamilton, Richard, 146
Hannity, Sean, 128
Hanson, Victor, 54
Hassan, Steven, 55, 105, 109
Hemphill, Pamela, 30
Hess, Jacob, 59
Hibbing, John, 56
Hitler, Adolf, 18, 21, 23, 78, 93–94, 114, 116, 132, 146
Hoover, Herbert, 108
Hutchinson, Cassidy, 55
identity politics, 90
January 6th, 28, 30, 55, 71, 92, 96, 106, 109
Kant, Immanuel, 14
Kelly, John, 144
Kennedy, John F., 71, 108
Konnikova, Maria 101
Landshut, 17–18
Machiavellianism, 104–105
Madoff, Bernie, 102–103
MAGA, 25, 106
mainstream media, 51, 115, 120, 131
Make America Great Again, 91, 119–120
manipulation of facts, 15

Massachusetts, 28
Matza, David, 61
MAXQDA, 41
McCain, John, 12
McCarthy, Joseph, 78–79
McRaney, David, 147
Melville, Herman, 100–101
Mesa, Arizona, 43, 52, 96, 121–122, 131, 136
Milgram Experiment, 19
Milgram, Stanley, 19
misinformation, 31–32, 38, 51, 105, 120, 128–132, 134–138, 143, 160, 162
Moore, Russell, 56
moral disengagement, 29, 60–63
moral justification, 62
moral rationalization, 44, 59–63, 65, 67, 69, 71, 123, 129
MSNBC, 12, 132, 171
Munich, 17
Mussolini, Benito, 93
narcissism, 53, 104, 114
national identity, 113
Nationalism, 50, 79
Nazi Germany, 61, 78, 114, 132, 154
Nazi Party, 94
Newsmax, 51, 92, 171
Norman, Oklahoma, 12
North Korea, 116, 154
Obama, Barak, 12
Oklahoma, 12, 26, 30, 36, 80, 82, 94, 107, 109, 120, 123, 131, 136, 153
Orbán, Viktor, 49, 79, 116
Palin, Sarah, 12
palliative comparison, 62
patriotism, 155
polarization, 57, 75, 96
political allegiance, 30, 35, 57, 74–75, 95, 146, 150, 152–154, 158–160
political culture, 32
political mobilization, 27
political tribalism, 76
Ponzi, Charles, 102–103
Populism, 49–50, 90
Populist movements, 49, 90, 93–94
Populist rhetoric, 50

propaganda, 14–15, 31, 93, 114–116, 132
Pryor, Oklahoma, 30, 82, 94, 107, 109, 120, 123, 121
psychological manipulation, 55
Psychopathy, 104–105
Rees, Brian, 55
Republican Party, 27, 48–50, 84–85, 90, 92, 106, 145, 169
Richfield, Utah, 31, 42
RINOs, 145
Roosevelt, Teddy, 22
Russia, 92, 116, 131–132
Russian, 92, 116
Schaller, Tom 55
Schutzstaffel, 14
South Carolina, 26–28, 36, 50, 93
southern border, 21
SS, 14, 18
St. George, Utah, 44, 81, 110
Stalin, Joseph, 116
Stanford prison experiment, 19
Stanley, Jason, 19, 88, 90
stolen election, 96, 167
Stop the Steal, 28
strongman, 15, 113, 117, 119–120, 122, 124–125, 156
Supreme Court, 169
Swan, Penny, 106
Sykes, Gresham, 61
Tajfel, Henri, 74
Tennessee, 28
Third Reich, 20–21
Thompson, William, 100
Tocqueville, Alexis de, 117–119
Totalitarianism, 9, 15–16, 114, 124
Tribalism, 73–81, 83, 85, 153, 156
Truman, Harry, 64
Trump, Donald 16, 21–23, 25–32, 36–39, 42–45, 47–57, 59, 62–72, 74, 76, 79–81, 83–85, 87–97, 104–111, 116, 119–125, 127, 131–134, 137, 140, 144–145, 149–155, 159, 167–168, 173
Trump Derangement Syndrome, 66, 139, 146–148, 154–156, 161–164, 166
Twain, Mark, 13

United States, 21, 23, 26, 48–49, 57, 69, 78–79, 82, 116, 120, 140, 150, 155, 163, 166, 168
University of Oklahoma, 12
Utah, 26, 31–32, 36, 42, 44, 51, 53, 81, 83, 88, 91, 110, 122–123, 151, 158
Venezuela, 155
victim blaming, 65
victim mentality, 111
victimhood, 27, 30, 44, 76, 87–97, 122, 125
Volkan, Vamik, 91
Waldman, Paul 55
Washington, D.C., 169
Washington, George, 21, 169
Weimar, 13–14, 94, 114
White House, 55, 127
YouTube, 134, 170
Zajonc, Robert, 104,

www.ingramcontent.com/pod-product-compliance
Lightning Source LLC
Chambersburg PA
CBHW020542030426
42337CB00013B/946